Nuclear Fallacies: How We Have Been Misguided since Hiroshima

The world changed irrevocably after Hiroshima, in ways we are only now beginning to understand. Our perceptions of life have been dramatically altered. The polemics of various factions around the nuclear issue often serve only to obscure further the realities of life in the nuclear age.

In a thoughtful and dispassionate reflection on the nuclear issue, Robert Malcolmson identifies a number of myths which society has come to accept:

- that the military does not really want nuclear war;
- that deterrence is an effective strategy for controlling nuclear confrontation;
- that United States nuclear superiority in the Cold War prevented a Soviet takeover of the West.

One by one these myths are explored and ultimately discredited. The truth of the nuclear issue emerges as a disturbingly different reality from what Western society believes.

"One of the most refreshing essays I have read. It confronts many of the basic difficult issues straight on and deals with them knowledgeably ... raises fundamental questions and answers them perceptively." Martin Sherwin, Tufts University, author of *A World Destroyed: The Atomic Bomb and the Grand Alliance*.

Robert W. Malcolmson teaches history at Queen's University in Kingston, Ontario.

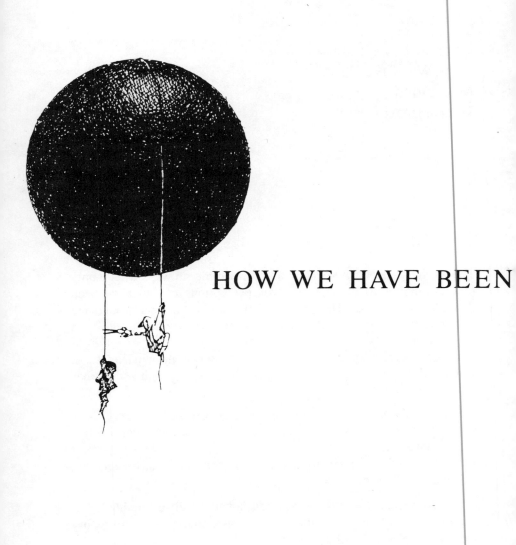

HOW WE HAVE BEEN

NUCLEAR FALLACIES

MISGUIDED SINCE HIROSHIMA

Robert W. Malcolmson

McGill-Queen's University Press

Kingston and Montreal

© McGill-Queen's University Press 1985
ISBN 0-7735-0585-7 (cloth)
ISBN 0-7735-0586-5 (paper)
Bibliothèque nationale du Québec
Legal deposit second quarter 1985
Printed in Canada

Paperback edition reprinted 1986

Designed by
Kok Kwan Shum

Canadian Cataloguing in Publication Data
Malcolmson, Robert M.
  Nuclear fallacies

  Bibliography: p.
  Inlcudes index.
  ISBN 0-7735-0585-7 (bound). – ISBN 0-7735-0586-5 (pbk.).

  1. Atomic weapons. 2. World politics – 1945–
  I. Title.

  U264.M34 1985   327.1'74   C85-098372-X

Publication has been assisted by the Canada Council and the
Ontario Arts Council under their block grant programs.

The cartoon by Jules Stauber on page ii is reproduced by kind permission of
Deutscher Taschenbuch Verlag GmbH & Co. KG. Munich.

For Pat and Stuart

Contents

Preface

"We have made a thing, a most terrible weapon, that has altered abruptly and profoundly the nature of the world."[1] These words were spoken in November 1945, just three months after Hiroshima, by J. Robert Oppenheimer, the scientific director of the Los Alamos laboratory where the first atomic bombs were designed and assembled. Many others – especially scientists, but also some observers of politics and even a few politicians – expressed similar views. They recognized that the destructive power of these new weapons was without precedent, and that, with their awesome appearance on the political scene, some of the basic assumptions governing the conduct of international relations would inevitably be called into question. The atomic bomb, it was agreed, was undeniably a revolutionary weapon; it marked a new departure in the world of power politics; and its implications were likely to penetrate into all aspects of experience. But would these implications be properly appreciated? Would some kind of rethinking of politics emerge in response to the revolutionary breakthroughs of science? These essential questions, which were already on some men's minds in 1945, have become a permanent part of our political culture, pressing us to face dilemmas and realities never before encountered. The distinguished writer on politics, the late Hans Morgenthau, put the point well when he observed that

> The nuclear age has ushered in a novel period of history, as distinct from the age that preceded it as the modern age has been from the Middle Ages or the Middle Ages have been from antiquity. Yet while

our conditions of life have drastically changed under the impact of the nuclear age, we still live in our thoughts and act through our institutions in an age that has passed. There exists, then, a gap between what we think about our social, political, and philosophic problems and the objective conditions which the nuclear age has created.[2]

Morgenthau's remarks capture the essence of the chapters that follow. For this is a work that is concerned to identify both the actual changes in the objective realities of life in the nuclear age and the various ways in which these realities have been perceived and misperceived. It considers, then, both man's new technologies and his efforts to manage and understand these technologies, especially as they relate to war and peace. It is both historical and contemporary in its perspectives; for throughout its pages I have tried to cast some light on both our immediate presence in the nuclear age and how we arrived at where we now are. Essentially it is a work of interpretation and synthesis: a work that considers some of what has been thought and done in the nuclear age and tries to interpret the politics of the nuclear arms race and to situate these weapons in the international culture of the past forty years.

It is also rather more than this. For while my purpose is primarily to explain and interpret, there is a sense in which this book is also an exercise in hope. It is an attempt, in part, in response to our present precariousness, to contribute to a clearer understanding of our nuclear predicament and to find grounds for the making of a more acceptable future. From the earliest days of the nuclear age there has been a persistent undertone of pessimism, foreboding, sometimes despair – a feeling of powerlessness in the face of our own destructive creations. As an observant Canadian diplomat, Escott Reid, wrote sombrely in October 1945, "The world of the atomic bomb presents problems which we seem incompetent to deal with."[3] This fear has been expressed, with varying degrees of intensity, ever since. But whatever pessimism one might feel, and however depressed one might sometimes become, it is vital to resist fatalism. The future is always at least partly open. Options remain, choices will be made, and alternative courses of action will contend for support. The actions that are taken, we might hope, will be more judicious than they might otherwise be if the ideas and memories that inform them are rendered as clear and as uncontaminated by stock responses as we can make them. It is to this end, in part, that the following pages are directed.

This book has benefited from the conversations I have had and the comments I have received from a number of people. Various friends and colleagues read the manuscript, in whole or in part, and I am grateful for their advice, criticism, and suggestions for change. I would mention in particular Boris Castel, Patricia Malcolmson, Joan McGilvray, Kerry McSweeney, Kevin Quinn, Larry Shore, Nancy Sutherland, and Nell and Dennis Waldman. Donald Akenson of McGill-Queen's University Press has been very helpful in smoothing the path towards publication; I have had several occasions to value his aid and encouragement. Several passages of this book first appeared in an essay in the *Queen's Quarterly*, Spring 1983; I appreciate the interest that the *Quarterly*'s editor, Michael Fox, showed in my work at that time. Grants from the Advisory Research Committee at Queen's University and the Ontario Arts Council helped to support my studies in 1983–4 and I am grateful for this tangible assistance. Catherine Frost edited the manuscript with admirable care and sensitivity.

... the future, which has so many elements of high promise, is yet only a stone's throw from despair.

J. Robert Oppenheimer, 26 August 1945

Has science fastened upon our society a monstrous gift of destruction which we can neither undo nor master, and which, like a clockwork automaton in a nightmare, is set to break our necks?

Jacob Bronowski, *Science and Human Values*, 1958

... all that alien hardware is
Ourselves wheeling about ourselves.

E.P. Thompson, "Prayer for the Year's Turning," 1983

1

A New Age

"… a searing light"

The definitive demonstration of man's ability to tap the energy released from nuclear fission occurred on 16 July 1945, before dawn, in the Alamogordo desert of New Mexico. At 5:30 that morning, while darkness still hung over the sands, a small group of men, both soldiers and civilian scientists, observed the experimental culmination of almost three years of intensive labour: the detonation, for the first time in history, of a nuclear device. Since the fall of 1942 the United States had been engaged in a massive undertaking which came to be known as the "Manhattan Project." It had been launched primarily out of fear of Nazi Germany – fear that the Nazis might have already embarked on a program to build nuclear bombs, and fear that unless the Anglo-American allies took immediate action to counter this possibility, they could expect only the worst. The American project that took shape (the United Kingdom and Canada were junior partners) was on the grand scale. It came to employ, at different times and in various ways, tens of thousands of people. It resulted in the building of entire new towns. It cost the staggering sum (by the standards of the 1930s) of 2.2 billion dollars. It consumed the energies of many of the world's finest scientific minds. It was the largest and most complex technological venture that the world had ever seen. In the light of these superlatives, it is remarkable that the entire project was carried out in the utmost secrecy. (Harry Truman did not know of it when he became president on 12 April 1945.) The results of all these efforts – scientific, industrial, military, organizational – were finally made manifest, at least to those few people with the requisite security clearance (the rest of mankind had to await the news from Hiroshima), on that mid-July morning at a remote location some 150 miles south of Albuquerque.

And what, exactly, did these men observe? The first thing they saw was an extraordinary brightness – a brightness beyond anything that any of them had ever before witnessed. "Suddenly and without any sound," recalled Otto Frisch, one of the British scientists at the test site, "the hills were bathed in brilliant light, as if somebody had turned on the sun with a switch."[1] Another recorder of the explosion was William L. Laurence, a science writer for the *New York Times* who had been appointed by the Manhattan Project to report, at a later date, on its various activities. Laurence's journalistic background did not fail him when he came to describe his sensations. At 5:30 a.m., he wrote:

> there rose as if from the bowels of the earth a light not of this world, the light of many suns in one. It was a sunrise such as the world had never seen, a great green supersun climbing in a fraction of a second to a height of more than eight thousand feet, rising ever higher until it touched the clouds, lighting up earth and sky all around with dazzling luminosity.
>
> Up it went, a great ball of fire about a mile in diameter, changing colors as it kept shooting upward, from deep purple to orange, expanding, growing bigger, rising as it expanded, an elemental force freed from its bonds after being chained for billions of years.[2]

The official report on the morning's events that was sent to Henry Stimson, the secretary of war, who read it to President Truman, was in its tone less intense and more matter of fact, but in its own way just as impressive. Stimson was told that the explosive power of the test was equivalent to at least 15,000 to 20,000 tons of TNT. "The light from the explosion was seen clearly at Albuquerque, Santa Fe, ... El Paso and other points generally to about 180 miles away." One of the distant witnesses "was a blind woman who saw the light."[3]

This awesome brightness was observed in silence. For a long time there was no sound at all. Then came the blast wave, the hot wind, the thunderous roar, the rumblings of the earth. A few observers also noticed the clouds of radioactive dust, and the strange way they glowed as they climbed up into the atmosphere.

The observers of this first nuclear explosion not only described what happened. They also reflected on its meaning and import, for humanity and for the future. While some, as one might expect, were simply gratified with the technical success of their venture and content that the massive effort to construct a nuclear bomb had paid off, others were more contemplative and sensitive to some of the human implications of the sudden appearance on the world's stage of such unprecedented power. Their reflections tended to be articulated within the tradition of religious expression, a kind of sensibility that seemed particularly appropriate to the drama and spectacle of the occasion. Joseph Hirschfelder, one of the scientists present, thought that "There weren't any agnostics watching this stupendous demonstration. Each, in his own way, knew that God had spoken."[4] Brigadier-General Thomas Farrell, the deputy military director of the entire Manhattan Project, even in his satisfaction at the success of the test, had certain doubts about what had been accomplished. Nuclear fission, he wrote, "was a great new force to be used for good or for evil." But as "the strong, sustained, awesome roar" of the explosion reached his shelter, some 10,000 yards from the point of the detonation, he could not help wondering – and his words were included in the War Department's official report – whether this roar "warned of doomsday"; for it "made us feel," he said, "that we puny things were blasphemous to dare tamper with the forces heretofore reserved to The Almighty."[5] Perhaps the most pertinent and most compelling reflection came from J. Robert Oppenheimer, a man of both scientific brilliance and humanistic refinement. At the moment that the blinding light lit up the desert, there flashed into Oppenheimer's mind a passage from the sacred book of the Hindus, the *Bhagavad-Gita*. The lines were as follows:

> If the radiance of a thousand suns
> Were to burst at once into the sky,
> That would be like the splendor
>   of the Mighty One ...
> I am become Death,
> The shatterer of worlds.

Science and Power

While the reality of nuclear power was decisively demonstrated only in the summer of 1945, we should not assume that it – or something rather like it – had not been imagined and foreseen in earlier years. In fact, a few prescient thinkers had already predicted a time when humanity would have vast new powers at its command and would have to face the task of managing these powers. Perhaps the most remarkable of these previews of nuclear power came from the fertile mind of H.G. Wells, in a novel written just before the First World War and first published in 1914, *The World Set Free*. Wells drew attention to the increasing human ability to exploit the energy of nature, and he anticipated that this long and accelerating process of technological advance would culminate with the splitting of the atom and the release of tremendous energy as a result of this fission. He foresaw that the most dramatic implication of nuclear energy would be its capacity to transform the character of warfare. And he conceived of future, large-scale warfare as being, pre-eminently, air war: war in which control of the air, and destruction from the air, would dominate the course of hostilities. But he was most concerned to explore the consequences for human society and political institutions of this future technology, especially for the relations among nation states. One of the participants in and observers of the first war in which nuclear weapons were used is made to say: "The atomic bombs had dwarfed the international issues to complete insignificance. When our minds wandered from the preoccupations of our immediate needs, we speculated upon the possibility of stopping the use of these frightful explosives before the world was utterly destroyed. For to us it seemed quite plain that these bombs and the still greater power of destruction of which they were the precursors might quite easily shatter every relationship and institution of mankind."[6] (Wells's proposed solutions to this plight were through world government.)

By 1939 the idea of nuclear fission had moved well beyond the realm of science fiction. During the winter of 1938–9 it had been scientifically proved and publicly revealed. What was still in doubt was the practical relevance of the new discovery. Was it technically possible to exploit the energy of the atom's nucleus for human purposes? As the Second World War broke out it seemed to many knowledgeable people that urgent efforts ought to be made to pursue the new prospects for energy, largely because of their possible military applications. This fervour within the scientific community was remarked on by the British scientist, writer, and public servant C.P.

Snow, in an editorial published in the journal *Discovery* in September 1939, just as war was declared. Snow could see the outlines of a new age emerging:

> Some physicists think that, within a few months, science will have produced for military use an explosive a million times more violent than dynamite. It is no secret; laboratories in the United States, Germany, France and England have been working on it feverishly since the Spring. It may not come off. The most competent opinion is divided upon whether the idea is practicable. If it is, science for the first time will at one bound have altered the scope of warfare. The power of most scientific weapons has been consistently exaggerated; but it would be difficult to exaggerate this.

What humanity was facing, Snow said, "is the old dream of the release of intra-atomic energy, suddenly made actual at a time when most scientists had long discarded it." And if this energy can actually be released, he asked – and others were raising the same question – how is the world likely to be affected? "What will happen, if a new means of destruction, far more effective than any now existing, comes into our hands? I think," he answered, that "most of us ... are pessimistic about the result. We have seen too much of human selfishness and frailty to pretend that men can be trusted with a new weapon of gigantic power ... In our time, at least, life has been impoverished, and not enriched, by the invention of flight. We cannot delude ourselves that this new invention will be better used." Such pessimism was not, however, to deter scientists from pressing on, if only because of the war that had just begun. In Snow's view, the nuclear bomb "must be made, if it really is a physical possibility. If it is not made in America this year, it may be next year in Germany. There is no ethical problem; if the invention is not prevented by physical laws, it will certainly be carried out somewhere in the world. It is better, at any rate, that America should have six months' start."[7]

In fact, the United States started slowly. But once it got started, it moved with speed and determination. And, most important, it finished first. The results of its extraordinary labours were communicated to the world at large, first at Hiroshima on 6 August 1945, and three days later at Nagasaki; on each occasion, a single B-29 bomber dropped its payload over the target city. Each bomb exploded at a height of about

2,000 feet. Each performed more or less according to plan. The total death toll in the two cities, including the delayed fatalities during the following six months, was at least 200,000 people.[8]

The bombings of Hiroshima and Nagasaki concentrated people's minds – or at least some people's minds – for they signalled a stunning and conspicuous transformation in the nature of warfare. Old modes of conduct and thinking suddenly demanded scrutiny. All the established rules of warfare, said some observers, would have to be re-examined, and many of these rules might have to be completely abandoned. As one strategic thinker later remarked, "with the advent of nuclear weapons the entire value of past military experience as a guide to the future was called basically into question."[9] Nuclear technology also forced people to confront, with a seriousness that had never before been so compelling, another fundamental problem: the role of science in modern society. The critical dimensions of this question were identified just after the end of the Second World War by Niels Bohr, the great Danish physicist. In 1946 Bohr published a short essay on "Science and Civilization" in which he touched on one of the central dilemmas of the modern condition:

> The possibility of releasing vast amounts of energy through atomic disintegration, which means a veritable revolution of human resources, cannot but raise in the mind of everyone the question of where the advance of physical science is leading civilization. While the increasing mastery of the forces of nature has contributed so prolifically to human welfare and holds out even greater promises, it is evident that the formidable power of destruction that has come within reach of man may become a mortal menace unless human society can adjust itself to the exigencies of the situation. Civilization is presented with a challenge more serious perhaps than ever before, and the fate of humanity will depend on its ability to unite in averting common dangers and jointly to reap the benefit from the immense opportunities which the progress of science offers.[10]

Bohr, like many prominent scientists, was something of an internationalist and advocated the strengthening of measures for collective action and the pursuit of co-operative endeavours among nations. While such aspirations have, thus far, remained largely unfulfilled, the problem that Bohr diagnosed is still very much with us and no closer to resolution.

The fear that technology might destroy the human race is not entirely novel: it has been represented by various strands of cultural pessimism concerning the impact of machines on men, attitudes of fear and antagonism that have persisted since at least the time of the Industrial Revolution. But these anxieties, which in previous generations were always dwarfed by the faith in progress, have become more deeply rooted, even if somewhat irregularly expressed, since 1945. For in the nuclear age we seem to approach the apotheosis of technology's ambiguous power. That is, we "possess" a technology that, in tapping the basic energy of the universe, threatens to turn on its human users and control them rather than be controlled. Nature, in a sense, no longer surrounds us; we surround it, both in our imaginations and in our actual power. But our control of this scientific power is an uncertain thing. Its presence, in the form of nuclear weaponry, is now pervasive and still growing. It looms over the conduct of that semi-anarchy known as international relations. It dominates much of our thinking about peace and the possibility of war. It threatens to make war into an experience totally unlike all previous human experiences. War, of course, is at the centre of our contemporary concerns; and it is to the nature of war and thinking about war in the nuclear age that our discussion now turns.

Technology and War

"War," observes Field Marshal Lord Carver, "is the final resort in the struggle for power."[11] It is the ultimate arbiter in relations between states. The making of war has, as we know, been a central reality in the ongoing pursuit of political ends; and the outcome of battle, and the nature of victory and defeat, have been undoubtedly affected, at various times and to various degrees, by the presence of new technologies. Certainly the custodians of sovereign power throughout the ages have been keenly interested in new military technologies – technologies that offered them improved capabilities for attacking enemies or for defending already-secured positions. Established weapons have been improved, new weapons have been invented. The crossbow, gunpowder, cannons on sailing ships, fast-loading rifles, heavy metal armaments, machine guns, aerial bombers – all these technological innovations have been enthusiastically adopted at various times in the past. Nuclear weaponry has sometimes been regarded as essentially the latest in a long line of breakthroughs in the technology of armaments, but this latest manifestation of force is a breakthrough of a new order of magnitude. For there are at least four major ways in which nuclear weapons are fundamentally different from those of all previous ages. These differences underlie and deeply reinforce the sense that we are, inescapably and undeniably, inhabiting a truly revolutionary age – that, as one of the scientists engaged in the Manhattan Project recalls feeling at the time of the Alamogordo test, "this was the end of one world and the beginning of another."[12] What, then, are these extraordinary implications of the weapons that now surround us?

First, nuclear weapons permit not merely the defeat of an adversary state, they make possible the total annihilation of that state and its society. Destruction can now be made virtually limitless – and essentially instantaneous. Distinctions between civilians and combatants, between military and non-military targets, are almost certain in any nuclear war to be largely or entirely meaningless. (One recalls that, in 1945, Hiroshima was regarded by American policy-makers as a centre of military importance, and was targeted partly for that reason.) Nuclear weapons, then, are not only vastly powerful, they are also by their very nature extremely blunt and undiscriminating instruments of destruction.

Second, not only is there no credible defence against nuclear weapons, it is virtually inconceivable that any such defence will ever exist. In order to inspire confidence, any plausible defence system would have to be essentially leakproof; for even if only a small fraction of an attacker's warheads were able to penetrate a defender's "shield," the resultant slaughter for that defender would be colossal. Moreover, defensive weapons are themselves vulnerable to attack, and it is difficult to see how even the most elaborate and sophisticated defence system could avoid being overwhelmed by sheer numbers, that is, by the addition of more and more offensive warheads to the arsenal of an adversary. Much thought has certainly been given, in military and engineering circles, to the possibility of constructing a defence against nuclear attack. But this thinking has led nowhere. Nor is it likely to yield fruit in the future. We are, in all likelihood, now at the end of the road in the long-standing struggle between offence and defence. Offensive force has triumphed definitively over defensive resistance. Universal vulnerability is now a fundamental fact of life.

Third, when nuclear weapons are possessed in abundance by at least two states, their use by any nuclear power is potentially suicidal. The first-use of nuclear weapons by one power will invite nuclear retaliation by another power, whether that initial use was "limited" and purportedly "restrained" or whether it was massive and pre-emptive in intent. In the former set of circumstances the momentum of warfare, the breakdown in communications, and the "fog of battle" are likely to make it extremely difficult for a nation's rulers to keep control of their huge nuclear arsenal and to prevent the conflict from becoming total; in circumstances of a pre-emptive attack, total war would exist from the start. Whatever the particular circumstances, the users of nuclear weapons risk destroying themselves along with their enemies.

Fourth, if nuclear weapons were used on a large scale, the natural environment might be so severely damaged that this planet would become largely uninhabitable – perhaps even totally uninhabitable – for most complex forms of life, our own species included. Here, of course, we are on very uncertain intellectual terrain. Our thinking about such matters is inevitably speculative. But many competent scientists have been studying the possible and likely consequences for our biosphere of varying levels of nuclear warfare, and the results of their inquiries point unequivocally to the manifold risks and dangers that would assuredly confront us. For we not only must think about the immediate destruction of life and those human institutions that have been built up over generations; we also have to consider the long-term implications for survival and recovery: the contamination of food and water supplies; the huge firestorms that would consume large areas; the probable spread of disease with the breakdown of public health; the collapse of agriculture in many regions because of the persistent cover of soot and dust clouds that would block out sunlight and cause a drop in temperature (a kind of "nuclear winter," whatever the season, with consequent widespread starvation); the possibility of long-term climatic changes resulting from damage to the protective atmosphere, especially the ozone layer.[13] The consequences of a major nuclear war could be with the world and its human survivors (let us assume some survivors) for centuries, perhaps even millennia. Nature is not likely to forgive quickly such an assault on its integrity.

The destructive possibilities here outlined are unique to the second half of this century. And it is clear that these possibilities are a consequence of the unrelenting industrialization of the means of making war. Machinery of increasing sophistication has been entering the armouries of nation states, with growing rapidity, for over a century. These machines have made killing much more efficient; they have allowed their possessors to fulfil the traditional objective of the soldier's enterprise – the successful application of force against opponents – with greater effect; and their presence in modern warfare has ensured that the casualties of battle are now much more numerous than ever before. Nuclear weapons, of course, are the most dramatic and starkly potent of the military products of industrialization. But even the non-nuclear weapons that are now with us – the fragmentation bombs, the undetectable mines, the guided missiles with deep-penetration capabilities – have achieved unparalleled levels of destructiveness. Conventional firepower in the twentieth century has taken tens of millions of lives. The consequences of this relentless process of industrialization compel us to face, as one distinguished historian has put it, "the dilemma of modern military power: that its destructiveness is now so great, in the conventional as well as the nuclear field, that its unleashing would certainly devastate what it is intended to preserve."[14]

We are pressed, then, by the technological realities that confront us, to consider seriously how they alter our traditional modes of thinking and conduct. In what ways have established ideas been transformed or even rendered obsolete? How have military strategists and the armed forces come to think about the new technologies under their command? And what are some of the unresolved difficulties in contemporary thinking about the role of nuclear weapons in international relations? These are the questions that dominate the rest of the discussion in this chapter.

Nuclear Strategy

In all previous ages weapons were made to be used as instruments of force in the pursuit of political objectives. Their utility was seldom questioned. Indeed, from the user's point of view, new weapons proved their worth on the battlefield. But nuclear weapons, with their vast destructive capacities – from blast, from fire, and from radiation – cannot be used with the sort of discrimination that was possible with previous armaments. They are not conducive to the selective applica-tion of force; rather, they threaten indiscriminate devastation. And what conceivable political objective, it has often been asked, could warrant such wholesale destruction? What possible ends could justify such means? Nuclear weapons, it is clear, subvert the long-established link between war and politics; for their use, rather than serving some political end, risks the obliteration of all human ends, political or otherwise. The rupture of this bond between military means and political ends was noticed by a few acute observers immediately after the end of the Second World War; they spoke of the emergence of "the absolute weapon," a weapon that transformed the rationale of all military power. One of these American commentators, Bernard Brodie, a student of politics and military strategy, said of the new age, in 1946, "[I am not] concerned about who will *win* the next war in which atomic bombs are used. Thus far the chief purpose of our military establishment has been to win wars. From now on its chief purpose must be to avert them. It can have almost no other useful purpose."[15]

Brodie's observation bristled with import, much of which came to be fully worked out and appreciated only in later years. It was an insight that pointed in a particular direction – a direction *away* from the conventions of all previous military thought. If we were to try to extract from Brodie's remarks the main implications for subsequent thinking about nuclear weapons, we could, I think, identify the following claims. (1) Nuclear war cannot be won. "Victory," in any conceivable form, is impossible in a nuclear war. Nuclear war cannot be fought, it can only be deterred. (2) In order to avert (or deter) future wars, the prime requirement is to be able to retaliate in kind to a nuclear attack. It is this capacity to retaliate that will (one hopes) deter a nuclear attack in the first place. (3) The ability to retaliate requires that any attack will not, even in the worst possible circumstances, be able to wipe out all a nation's nuclear arsenal. There must, then, be an assurance that some of this arsenal will be invulnerable in the face of even the most determined offensive. (This has now come to be known as a second-strike capability.) (4) International great-power relations must now be seen as a kind of stalemate, a balance of terror, an equilibrium sustained by fear. If this is so, it will be necessary to reject most of the deeply rooted dynamic dimensions of established military strategy – those assertive and take-charge aspects of strategy to which military professionals have been so deeply and for so long committed.

Here, then, in an early commentary on the significance of nuclear weaponry, one discerns the roots of that complex of ideas that would come to be known as the doctrine of deterrence. As a self-conscious theory it was systematically elaborated only in later years; however, its principal propositions were already taking shape very soon after the new weapons made their debut on the international stage. (New ideas about nuclear weapons are rare; innovation is almost entirely in the realm of technology, which so-called strategic thinking, most of which is funded by the military, does little more than justify and adapt itself to.) Some people have tried to spell out and explain the theory of nuclear deterrence with precision and clarity; more often, however, its meaning has been left vague and its practical implications have not been closely scrutinized. Its fuzziness, in fact, has been one of its main attractions for those who most commonly speak of it: government officials and spokesmen for "national security." Certainly, it is a notion that thas been repeatedly appealed to for over three decades, to explain the need for this new military base and that new sophisticated weapon, to justify both those new warheads (and their delivery systems) that are imminent and the requests for more funds to develop even newer weapons that will be deployed in, say, six to eight years. The language of deterrence, in these circles, commonly functions in a ritualized fashion. It is often repeated, though rarely examined closely. But whatever vagueness and elasticity might be embedded in its use, it clearly bears and is intended to bear a certain message. And that message, I think, as it has been apprehended by most of the public, is that nuclear warfare is, in some elemental sense, "unthinkable" and is being treated as such by those to whom power is entrusted, and that all responsible authorities are fully aware of the unique dangers and revolutionary realities of the nuclear age. "Deterrence," moreover, has the ring of benign intent: an intention merely to discourage aggression, to preserve order, to keep violent conflict at bay.

   In actual historical experience, in the circles that truly count – the military and bureaucratic elites – important chunks of deterrence thinking never became universally accepted. Indeed, it was always regarded, in certain respects, as decidedly unpalatable. The suggestion that nuclear war is fundamentally unthinkable has held little appeal for many military officers and strategists, who have in fact thought at length about nuclear weapons and have been determined to discover legitimate uses for them. They have incorporated these weapons into tactical battle plans; they have tried to be selective and discriminating in their targeting designs; and they have worked out war-fighting strategies in which nuclear weapons are used to achieve what they call victory. Among these influential military men and strategists, nuclear weapons have tended to be seen, in part, as extensions of conventional weapons, as weapons at one end of a continuum of usable fire-power. Indeed, many of these military planners have spoken of the possibility of "limited" nuclear wars, of "controlled" exchanges of nuclear strikes, of "flexible nuclear responses," of the need to achieve "escalation dominance," of "tolerable" casualty levels, and of the possibility of a rapid recovery from the anticipated damage caused by a well-managed nuclear conflict. Not all these strategists hold exactly the same views; there are different emphases and nuances of argument. But they are very much united in accepting the coercive utility of nuclear weapons and in asserting that these weapons can be satis-factorily incorporated into the doctrinal and operational traditions of the military forces. One of these strategists, Colin S. Gray, who has wielded some influence in Washington in the 1980s, believes that "there is a role for ... the sensible, politically directed application of military power in thermonuclear war," and he speaks of the need "to provide some overall political integrity to strategic [nuclear] planning."[16] Some of these "defence intellectuals" fear that the presence of nuclear technology has made the United States excessively timid in its attitudes to the use of force. As Gray and an associate have put it: "the West needs to devise ways in which it can employ strategic nuclear forces coercively, while minimizing the potentially paralyzing impact of self-deterrence. If American nuclear power is to support u.s. foreign policy objectives, the United States must possess the ability to wage nuclear war rationally."[17]

These particular views are unusual only in their explicitness. Such thinking is actually implicit, and sometimes openly stated (though little publicized), in much of the military planning that for years has pertained to both superpowers' expanding nuclear arsenals. For many military professionals and strategists, deterrence has come to have quite different connotations from those the broader public has come to accept. As Desmond Ball, an acute and knowledgeable Australian observer of these matters, has remarked, "the central concept in current u.s. strategic doctrine" is now that of "controlled escalation," a notion markedly unlike that mode of thinking that stresses the importance of ensuring a survivable retaliatory capability. He points out that "The notion of deterrence is still invoked, but it is now seen as involving much more than simply maintaining an unambiguous second-strike assured destruction capability ... as the spectrum of contingencies to be deterred has widened, so has the nature of the concept itself ... the capacity for nuclear war-fighting is now regarded as an essential ingredient of a successful deterrent."[18] The military establishment, in fact, has come to interpret deterrence in a very ambitious, virtually all-encompassing manner. Its plans for fighting a nuclear war are now highly elaborate. As Desmond Ball has concluded in another study of these matters, "the u.s. target plans for strategic nuclear war are now extremely comprehensive." Current strategic plans include more than 40,000 potential targets (most of them in the ussr), up from 25,000 in 1974, 3,260 in 1957, and 70 in the late 1940s. These targeting plans, notes Ball, are "designed to enhance the ability of the u.s. National Command Authorities to conduct limited and selective nuclear strikes and to control escalation so as to produce outcomes favourable to the u.s.."[19] The objective of these plans, in short, is to ensure that the United States will be dominant over the Soviet Union in any post-nuclear-war world.

War-planning, on an increasingly complex scale, has been a central characteristic of u.s. nuclear policy since the late 1940s, and these plans have been premised on the assumption – at least since the Soviet Union obtained its own substantial arsenal and thus could set some of the rules of play – that nuclear combat (normally referred to as "nuclear exchanges") can be conducted with restraint and prudence. Some of the recent critics of this war-planning heritage object to it, not because they feel that it is implausible, but rather on the grounds that it is not taken sufficiently seriously. That is, they fear that American policy-makers are not fully committed to the pursuit of nuclear victory. American policy, they feel, goes part way in the search for victory, but not all the way. As Colin S. Gray puts it, "the United States should not have an operational ... policy of being willing to initiate a very small nuclear war ... unless it has a very persuasive theory for the successful conduct of a very large nuclear campaign."[20] American nuclear policy, according to this view, has been much too inhibited; "u.s. official thinking and planning," complains Gray, "does not embrace the idea that it is necessary to try to effect the *defeat* of the Soviet Union." The fundamental purpose of u.s. military force should be clearly acknowledged: "The United States should plan to defeat the Soviet Union and to do so at a cost that would not prohibit u.s.

recovery. Washington should identify war aims that in the last resort would contemplate the destruction of Soviet political authority and the emergence of a postwar world order compatible with Western values ... Once the defeat of the Soviet state is established as a war aim, defense professionals should attempt to identify an optimum targeting plan for the accomplishment of that goal."[21]

Such views have not been confined to the margins of the American "national security" establishment. They have been taken very seriously by people of high authority. Richard Burt, just before he assumed a senior position in the State Department in 1981, advocated a revamped strategy of nuclear escalation. "A new emphasis," he said, "must be placed on generating nuclear responses that are militarily meaningful." He went on to call for "a broader concept for nuclear use" and for "American forces [that] are capable of waging a large scale, sustained nuclear campaign."[22] Such thinking has now become quite commonplace – at least in official circles. As two of its defenders put it in 1984, writing in a journal closely linked to the Pentagon (one of the authors had helped formulate U.S. nuclear targeting policy): "the U.S. concept of deterrence has matured. Deterrence is no longer deemed distinct from – or antagonistic to – the capabilities to conduct nuclear war operations. Current U.S. strategy recognizes that credible operational capabilities are essential to effective deterrence." This, they state, is the "concept of a deterrent based on an ability to conduct nuclear war."[23] Such assumptions about the possibility of waging a limited nuclear war have had a considerable impact on the changing agenda of U.S. strategy during the 1980s, as seen, for example, in the priority that has been given to plans for "prevailing" in a protracted, global nuclear contest with the USSR.

The emphasis in the thinking of many military planners has been, and still is, very much on the continuing relevance in the nuclear age of established military thinking and practice – a tradition whose principal concern is the pursuit of victory. These men tend to be ill at ease with views that stress the revolutionary and potentially suicidal implications of nuclear weaponry. For soldiers, weapons have always existed to be used. Given their existence, they should obviously be turned to some sort of advantage. To have weapons that exist *not* to be used is, for military men, a very strange state of affairs. Moreover, soldiering has always been an assertive and active profession, whose ultimate rewards are achieved on "the field of battle." A strict version of deterrence has not sat well with these traditions. As a retired U.S. admiral has pointed out: "Military men have always been unsatisfied with the limitations of a purely deterrent policy which strikes them as too passive, too inflexible, too limiting, too demoralizing, and even too immoral. Military men have wanted to make nuclear weapons manageable tools of warfare, weapons like any other weapons which can be used to prevail in battle over the enemy. Military men have always sought an edge and resisted the self-limitations of deterrence."[24]

From a military perspective, a strict version of deterrence is constrictively reactive. It has rather limited military appeal; for, if adhered to closely, "it results in a strategy which leaves all the initiative to the adversary and deprives the possession of nuclear weapons of any real political value: in a purely deterrent posture, nuclear weapons become useless as coercive implements."[25] Such self-deprivation has not been easy to swallow. Indeed, for the most part it has been firmly resisted. Whatever the declaratory policy of the armed forces has been – and it has always highlighted the deterring of war – the operational planning of these forces has been much less reticent about the actual use of all kinds of force, including the first-use of nuclear force in a variety of circumstances.

Nuclear war-fighting doctrines, it is clear, have been sturdily present since almost the beginning of the nuclear age, although their prominence in public and official discussions has tended to ebb and flow. The earliest strategies for the use of nuclear weapons arose out of the tradition of area bombing in the Second World War, and in the U.S. air force after 1945 nuclear bombs came to be regarded largely as a more efficient means of inflicting the same kind of devastation that had recently been visited on the cities of Germany and Japan. By the mid-1950s this heritage of strategic bombing, based on the superiority of command in the air, had achieved expression as the doctrine of "massive retaliation." All sorts of provocation, nuclear and non-nuclear, were seen as possible grounds for the use of U.S. nuclear bombs. The concern for fighting "limited" nuclear wars emerged shortly thereafter and has had its ups and downs among national security specialists ever since. Whenever these various doctrines have been espoused, they have almost always been defended as a way of "strengthening our deterrent" and of making war less likely. But how have these doctrines of possible nuclear use been related to the classic specifications of deterrence, as Bernard Brodie first formulated them? Is the one set of views compatible with the other? In order to examine these matters, it will be necessary both to clarify what deterrence has meant – indeed, what various meanings it has been given – and to identify what conditions of existence it ought and ought not to be allowed to represent.

Deterrence

Deterrence means, in strategic parlance, that no nuclear power would rationally choose to attack another such power because of the devastating consequences of unavoidable retaliation. As the Israeli diplomat Abba Eban has put it, "The logic of nuclear deterrence is fulfilled if a country possesses a measure of invulnerability for its retaliatory forces together with a capacity to inflict damage that an adversary in his right mind would find unacceptable."[26] Given an assured retaliatory capability, and given that no nuclear power has any confidence that it can seriously defend against a nuclear attack or counterattack, then no nuclear power has any incentive for launching a strike against any other nuclear power. Indeed, to do so would risk a counterblow of overwhelming force. In this way, it is hoped, a kind of perpetual stand-off may be brought about. This is the essence of deterrence. And, on the surface, it might seem to be fairly straightforward and perhaps even unproblematic. In fact, as a doctrine it is anything but straightforward. It is and has been riddled with problems and uncertainties, and in order to understand its complex character more precisely, we shall have to remark on some of its peculiarities, its internal contradictions, and its inherent limitations. What is it, then, about deterrence that warrants special notice?

First, while deterrence assumes at least two nuclear powers, and thus a *mutuality* in the relationship of terror, this mutuality did not actually exist during the first twenty years of the nuclear age. For although the USSR became a sort of nuclear state in 1949, it was only from the mid-1960s that it actually had a substantial capacity to launch a nuclear attack against its American adversary, either in a first-strike or in retaliation. Before that time American superiority was always overwhelming, and the Soviet intercontinental nuclear attack force was, even as late as the early 1960s, relatively feeble. One major result of this discrepancy in power was that the United States, recognizing the superiority of its advanced technology (nuclear and otherwise), and yet fearing the might of the Red Army and of "International Communism," deliberately chose to emphasize the role of its nuclear weapons as a means of achieving its diplomatic and political ends. (These ends were mostly embraced in the policy of "containment.") Nuclear weapons were seen in the United States as suitable not simply for retaliation against a nuclear attack (there was virtually no chance of such an attack). Rather, they were assigned a role of importance in deterring all sorts of perceived threats against American interests around the world. On some twenty occasions, most of them before the mid-1960s, the United States threatened, implicitly or explicitly, to use nuclear weapons as a coercive instrument in support of its policy objectives.[27] American policy, in other words, employed the "nuclear threat," which for many years only the United States could credibly make, in order to discourage the use of non-nuclear force by its enemies. Shows of nuclear force and the sending of nuclear signals were important dimensions of American diplomacy. It is clear, in fact, that American policy-makers had come to regard their rapidly growing nuclear arsenal as the centre-piece of the nation's pursuit of basic security.

All this ran counter to a strategy of strict deterrence. For the policies of these years tended to stress the utility, not the non-utility, of nuclear weapons. Because of the nuclear hegemony of the United States, American leaders were tempted to consider how their nuclear arsenal could be turned to political advantage and incorporated into a variety of war-fighting plans. They were certainly aware of constraints on the use of their nuclear weaponry (such as the ability of the Soviet army to retaliate against a U.S. attack by invading western Europe), but they felt much less constrained than they would have had the USSR possessed a roughly equivalent nuclear force. The essential mutuality of deterrence, then, was for many years lacking. One of the results of this period of obvious imbalance of nuclear power was that U.S. strategy became deeply committed, from very early in the nuclear age, to nuclear war-fighting doctrines, which held that nuclear weapons could be rationally managed and purposefully directed in the service of vital security interests, in peace or in war. (What lessons the Russians drew from these American doctrines – aside from being given grounds for great mistrust of American intentions – we do not know.) The objective foundation for a true mutuality of deterrence only became a firm reality a generation after Hiroshima; in short, what Bernard Brodie foresaw in 1945–6 took some twenty years to materialize. And during those years Brodie's original sense of deterrence was very much extended – extended to cover a fairly wide range of conflict situations, thereby undermining the decidedly self-limiting dimensions of a strict version of deterrence. The legacy of these war-fighting strategies is still very much with us, and the resilience of the exponents of these doctrines is demonstrated today in the writings of strategic experts, the recommendations of military planners, and the many extant plans for the conduct of "disciplined" nuclear warfare.

A second major point emerges from these remarks. It is this: However strictly the doctrine of nuclear deterrence has been defined, it has always tended to expand beyond these tight limits. It has been very difficult to contain it. Indeed, few professional strategists and military planners in the West have been prepared to regard it as a purely retaliatory doctrine, that is, as a doctrine that explicitly forgoes the claim to use nuclear weapons except in case of nuclear attack. The notion of deterrence has, in fact, been handled in a very elastic fashion. It has been stretched this way and that way to justify all sorts of actions. A telling illustration of this imprecision may be found in the 1983 report of the Scowcroft Commission, where deterrence is defined as follows: "Deterrence is the set of beliefs in the minds of Soviet leaders, given their own values and attitudes, about our capabilities and our will. It requires us to determine, as best we can, what would deter them from considering aggression, even in a crisis – not to determine what would deter us." Deterrence is thus reduced to being a state of mind.[28] But states of mind are, of course, very hard to know. And the minds of Soviet leaders would seem to be especially difficult to penetrate. Yet deterrence is here being made to rest on such shrouded and (at least in the eyes of the beholders) easily shifted sands. Almost anything can be imagined about the minds of others. Such a definition allows no more or less firm reference points or standards of assessment. It is, in fact, almost completely open-ended. It offers no way of knowing how much is enough (much less how much is too much), or what weapons to buy, or when deterrence has been satisfied. Like many exclusively psychological definitions of conflict relationships, just about anything can be read into it. And given this imprecision, virtually any new weapon system can be confidently defended on the grounds that it "strengthens our deterrent."

Like all offensive armaments, nuclear weapons are threatening, but it is not at all clear – and deterrence theory is very vague on this point – when the threat to use them should be made. Strict deterrence condones only the threat to retaliate against a nuclear attack. But most actual strategic usages of deterrence favour a much broader role for nuclear threats. According to one prominent strategist, deterrence is "the ability through the nuclear threat to make an opponent refrain from what he otherwise might do."[29] This allows a very large scope for strategic nuclear policy. Rather than determinedly striving to limit the utility of nuclear weapons, such a view encourages an enlargement of their political significance. And it is just this emphasis that has been expressed in the long-standing Western commitment to extended deterrence, that is, a concept of deterrence that asserts the willingness of the United States to use (or at least threaten to use) nuclear weapons in circumstances other than a clear-cut nuclear attack against its own national territory, or even that of an ally. Such an extension of the mission of the u.s. nuclear deterrent – an extension well beyond the doctrinal framework that Bernard Brodie had outlined – has been the norm, not the exception, in Western strategic doctrine.

There is a third characteristic of deterrence that warrants comment. It has been remarked on by numerous observers, who note that, strictly speaking, deterrence is not a strategy at all. Rather, it is a way of ensuring that existing weapons will not be used under any circumstances. As one writer has put it, "Deterrence teaches nothing about the manner in which nuclear weapons may be employed. It is, rather, a device to make their employment unnecessary. In this sense it is the very opposite of strategy. It provides only for before the war."[30] As Bernard Brodie had indicated, the point of military force was now to avert war, not to conduct it. But, as so many strategists have been keen to ask, what if deterrence fails? What if, during some international crisis, or at a time of internal upheaval in some nuclear-armed state, the reciprocal fear that supposedly sustains stability in the nuclear age momentarily falters and, for whatever reason, some state initiates a nuclear attack? If this were to happen, what should we do? (It is normally assumed in these scenarios that it is "we" who are attacked by "them.") How should we respond? What plans should be made for this eventuality? It is at this point in the logic of military thinking – the presumed breakdown of peace – that strategists become really interested in their work. For a strict approach to deterrence downplays the importance of classical strategy ("the pursuit of victory"), stresses the non-utility of modern weaponry, and allows military planners relatively little room for professional and intellectual manoeuvre. Strict deterrence, in other words, casts doubt on the whole enterprise of elaborately worked out strategies for war, especially nuclear war. It implies that such strategies may no longer make much sense. It suggests that we may now inhabit a world in which strategy, at least as applied to nuclear weapons, is largely anachronistic. One should hardly be surprised that this proposition has not met with general approval in the various military establishments. Indeed, a constant concern of many military professionals has been to incorporate all forms of modern military technology within those war-fighting traditions that have existed from time immemorial, while at the same time making use of a new rhetoric – the elastic rhetoric of deterrence – to suggest publicly, and perhaps even to themselves, that the wars they are planning are never likely to take place.

One sees, then, that a fundamental tension underlies deterrence, a tension that is rooted in the actual presence, in abundance, of weapons of such vast destructive power. For while we may be intent on preventing them from being used, the fact is that, simply because they exist, they could be used. And if they could be used, some men will turn their minds to wondering how they might be used. And in planning for their possible use they inevitably scare people in other nations, who plan how they, too, might possibly "have to" use the nuclear weapons under their command. Such contingency planning becomes, over time, increasingly elaborate and sophisticated; it also feeds on mutual fears, with each side suspecting and becoming alarmed about the war plans of the other side – but not, of course, alarmed about its own. All this imagining goes on in the realm of possibilities. But there is always the inherent danger that possibilities, when built very deeply into the operational structures of vast military machines, may some day, during a crisis, be quickly transformed into probabilities. Plans start to be carried out. First steps are taken. Forces go on alert. Tensions become acute. At a time such as this all those plans for the use of nuclear weapons, made in the name of deterrence, are in danger of generating their own momentum, of capturing the thoughts of political and military leaders, and of hindering whatever counter-efforts might be under way – efforts for staving off a cataclysmic conflict. In this way, then, the planning for nuclear war heightens the risk of war, even if this planning is carried out (as it almost always is) in the name of deterrence. And the result is that the substance of deterrence, rather than being strengthened, is actually undermined and enfeebled.

Doubts and Doubters

Rear Admiral Gene LaRocque has recently written some harsh words about deterrence, or at least the way in which the notion of deterrence is so commonly tossed around. It is, he says, "such a vague term that it can be used, and has been used, to justify everything we do. It is now purely a slogan. It has no real value as either a guide to what we *should* do or to what we actually do in our policy toward the Soviet Union." He questions, then, whether it conveys any clear and useful meaning. And he points to some of the ways in which it has become twisted and abused. "Deterrence," he suggests, "has been a useful concept for public relations purposes because it sounds good, just as the word 'defense' sounds good."[31] Undoubtedly it retains much rhetorical and tranquillizing utility. Its meaning has become so imprecise and so readily manipulated that it can now be used by anyone to "explain" almost anything. Certainly it is much appealed to in the everyday, opportunistic political war of words that regularly surrounds us. Whether or not deterrence is in any way intellectually valid and how it might actually bear on our understanding of global political realities in the nuclear age are questions that are still very much under active discussion.

Considered from a long historical perspective, the notion of deterrence is, of course, hardly new. States have been committed to such retaliatory practices for centuries. But in the past retaliation often made manifest sense: if an adversary were not deterred, victory in war was readily conceivable and often attainable, and thus retaliatory action was by no means irrational. This, however, is no longer the case – or at least it is very unlikely to be so. Modern instruments of destruction have probably rendered the traditional concept of victory obsolete; when catastrophe attains unprecedented heights, the ancient distinction between victor and vanquished is almost sure to be meaningless. The new realities of the nuclear world have been remarked on by numerous observers, among them Field Marshal Lord Carver, a former chief of the British defence staff. The acute dilemma of our age, he writes, is that "if you wish to deter war by the fear that nuclear weapons will be used, you have to appear to be prepared to use them in certain circumstances. But if you do so, and the enemy answers back – as he has the capability to do and has clearly said he would – you are very much worse off than if you had not done so, if indeed you can be said to be there at all. To pose an unacceptable risk to the enemy automatically poses the same risk, or perhaps an even greater one, to yourself."[32]

Here, indeed, is one of the critical elements of our modern predicament. Any use of nuclear weapons, under any circumstances, threatens to be suicidal. Anything but the unqualified *non-use* of these weapons, indefinitely observed by both – or, perhaps in the future, all – great powers, raises the prospect of both self-annihilation and general devastation. And because of this prospect we hope to achieve the immobilization of nuclear aggression through universal terror. All nations are afraid, and thus, it is hoped, all will be prudent. It is also hoped that this prudence will persist indefinitely; that is, that deterrence will be permanently effective, and that nuclear weapons, even as they become increasingly elaborate, will remain permanently unused. In contrast to the deterrent practices in the past, as Brodie pointed out in 1959, "the policy of deterrence we are talking about today is markedly different in several respects. For one thing, it uses a kind of threat which we feel must be *absolutely* effective, allowing for no breakdown whatever. The sanction is, to say the least, not designed for repeating action. One use of it will be fatally too many."[33] While deterrence depends on the ability to retaliate, actually to do so would signal the total failure of public policy and perhaps the total collapse of social life. "In the pre-nuclear age," as Hans Morgenthau once pointed out, "the threat and the counterthreat of force could always be, and frequently were, put to the test of actual performance, and either the threat or the counterthreat was then proved to be empty. In the nuclear age, the very purpose of threat and counterthreat is to prevent the test of actual performance from taking place."[34] Before the nuclear age deterrence "acquired relevance and strength from its failures as well as its successes."[35] However, such tolerance of failure is no longer possible. For the price of failure – even one instance of failure – now defies rational calculation.

There is, clearly, a disturbing tension in the modern doctrine of deterrence, a tension between posture (that is, the declaration of nuclear threats) and practice (that is, making good on these threats). This tension is nicely highlighted in a remark by a French political commentator. "Compared with other armaments," he asserts, "atomic weapons have the advantage ... that using them is so risky that those who have them are afraid to resort to them. The other weapons are intended to kill, these to intimidate."[36] But can killing and intimidation really be so readily dissociated? How can weapons intimidate if others think, or even strongly suspect, that they will not be used? Intimidation, to be credible, must be backed up by a disposition, at some time or other, to unleash these weapons, to use them fully, just as other weapons have been used in the past. Otherwise it would be merely a policy of bluff. But to use these weapons would mean that the policy that had justified their acquisition, the policy of deterrence, had transparently failed. And once deterrence fails, if it fails, for whatever reason (and no doubt each side will see itself as reacting to the provocative initiatives of the other side), we are greatly in danger of finding ourselves in a situation that calls for action leading to mutual suicide.

This is an unprecedented situation. Never before have the potential costs of carrying out a threat been so staggering. Never before has there been such a striking dissonance between, on the one hand, the logic of stated intention – that is, the assurance of retaliation – and, on the other hand, the irrationality of this promised conduct if it were actually to be pursued. Striking back holds out virtually no prospect for making things better, or for reversing a setback, or for retrieving the initiative, or for mitigating losses already suffered. Deterrence thinking, as Jonathan Schell points out, has "endeavoured to increase the element of *threat* to the maximum while reducing the risk of *use* to the minimum." This effort, he claims – and the claim is hard to refute – was, essentially, self-contradictory, "since the threat was credible only insofar as use was a real possibility"; it was "like trying to make use of the shadow of an object without having the object itself," to threaten, and thereby to achieve certain benefits, but never to act upon these threats. We find ourselves, in short, in a rather absurd situation, a situation that is rooted in the very existence of nuclear arsenals, which doctrine then tries to rationalize and render intelligible. To obtain the benefit of a posture of deterrence, according to Schell, "we must threaten to perform an insane action. But the benefit we seek is precisely *not* to perform that action. We thus seek to avoid performing an act by threatening to perform it."[37] It is hard to imagine that we can rest content with these contortions indefinitely.

As yet there is little sign that governments are much given to sceptical views on the doctrine of deterrence. Indeed, they propose huge expenditures in the name of this doctrine. Undoubtedly it would be utopian, and perhaps even foolish, to expect the great powers, in the present state of world affairs, to renounce the retaliatory core of nuclear deterrence. But we should not conceal from ourselves the confused thinking that surrounds this commitment to nuclear retaliation. As Herbert Butterfield, a distinguished historian and Christian thinker, once remarked in questioning the justification for this threat, "the right of retaliation could mean no more than the right to multiply an initial catastrophe that could not be undone."[38] If deterrence ever does fail, probably the only sensible thing to do would be to try to stop the whole debacle as soon as possible; that is, quickly to restore diplomatic communications, to pull back from the brink, to resist demands for urgent military action, and to seek as the foremost priority the termination of hostilities. Efforts of this sort, efforts to regain political control of a desperate and potentially ruinous situation, would, in virtually any conceivable circumstances, be much more rational than a nuclear response to an emerging conflict. If the principal objective of war is to bring about a better peace, it seems clear that nuclear retaliation as a means to attain this political end is, to say the least, neither entirely convincing, nor rich in promise, nor free of contradictions.

In considering these matters we should take pains, I think, to distinguish between the various doctrines concerning deterrence, which are seriously flawed, and what we might call the existential reality of deterrence. Existential deterrence arises inescapably from the mere existence of nuclear weapons: given their existence, they *could* be used. This is not a theory; it is simply an elementary fact of life. Moreover, whatever may happen to the world's nuclear arsenals in the future, and even if they can be substantially reduced, the scientific knowledge that underlies this weaponry will always be with us, ready to be converted into warheads at any time. In this sense an early interpreter of nuclear age, Hanson Baldwin, the military correspondent of the *New York Times*, was undoubtedly right when he said in 1947 that "The awful weapons man has created are now forever with us; we shall walk henceforth with their shadow across the sun."[39]

Here is the central core of existential deterrence that we have to face up to. Because of our understanding, because of what we have learned, we are destined to live in the shadow of nuclear weapons, in some way or other, forever. Knowledge, it has been said, is power; and knowledge now gives us the power to destroy ourselves. Since this knowledge cannot be erased, we shall have to find ways of coming to terms with it, of managing it intelligently, of not letting it get the better of us. This, as Jonathan Schell has observed, is the new state of nature in which we find ourselves.[40] We cannot wriggle out of it. But we can at least try to deal realistically with these new facts of life, to understand them as clearly as possible, and to seek ways to reduce the risks that are inherent in our new condition of existence. And in working out these strategies for survival we shall have to strip away from the idea of deterrence all those outdated, foggy, and sometimes incoherent notions that have grown up around it over the years. Much of the theorizing about deterrence is arid, convoluted, ideological, and pointless; and in many cases it is simply a cover for planning the conduct of nuclear war – the sort of war that is likely to lead only to the grave. The fallacies in these doctrines need to be exposed. But even if and when they are, we shall not be let off the nuclear hook. For as long as any nuclear weapons exist, their use is possible; and as long as people exist in a state of knowledge, these weapons can always be made. Managing our knowledge and our capacities, then, in the interest of common survival, will remain permanently on the agenda of public life.

Is Control Possible?

Let us conclude with one final observation – an observation that touches on a critical dimension of our thinking about nuclear weapons. The more one examines what others have thought about these weapons, and the more one inspects the official and unofficial thinking about our existence in the nuclear age, the more it is apparent that much of this thinking revolves around one large, fundamental issue: that is, the question of *manageability*. For the first time in history we face the prospect that what we have created may not be within our powers of control. The sheer destructiveness of our new technology threatens to break through and overwhelm those human institutions that are designed to contain violence, to civilize human relations, and to preserve the continuity of life. If this technology were applied to the actual conduct of war, there is the distinct possibility that war would cease to be, as it has heretofore always been, a means to an end, and become instead an end in itself, perhaps even the absolute end. Man's technology has now transformed the very significance of warfare. Nuclear technology is manifestly so potent in relation to its human creators that it could easily run away with us. It confers upon us a power that we may not be able to control. Indeed, it is most dramatically through this technology that science, as one observer has put it, "threatens to transform itself from the servant to the executioner of mankind."[41]

It is on this question of control that one detects a striking incompatibility between the dominant orthodox military thinking since 1945 and the thinking of those who are mostly outside the various military establishments. Military doctrine has assumed that nuclear weapons can be controlled. It has been determined to find ways in which this new technology can be made politically usable. It has rejected the proposition that nuclear weaponry has rendered obsolete the objectives of classical strategy, including the pursuit of victory. As one writer has observed, "Since the dawn of the nuclear age, the military mind has been at work trying to devise plausible scenarios for nuclear-war-fighting in which traditional operational considerations, such as numerical superiority, the importance of offensive momentum, the relevance of defense, and even the possibility of victory, all play a part."[42] Strategic thinkers have been intent on finding ways in which nuclear weapons could be employed, at least by means of threats, to alter the conduct of other states. They have worked diligently to devise plans for the "rational" use of these weapons. They have stressed, not the fundamental discontinuities between the nuclear and the pre-nuclear age, but rather the political continuities and the enduring relevance in the nuclear age of the heritage of strategic thought. A representative expression of this outlook can be found in a remark by two American writers on international politics, Robert Art and Kenneth Waltz, who assert that "nuclear power, though revolutionary in the magnitude of its destructive force and in the speed of its deliverability, is nevertheless still only an instrument of force – usable to threaten and deter, to punish and destroy. And these are the ways in which force in the hands of rulers has always been used."[43]

Such assumptions as to the political utility of nuclear weapons have been commonplace among military strategists and policy-makers. They reject the proposition that man has now been dwarfed by his own military creations. As one authority has remarked, in concluding a detailed history of the development of American strategic thought, "The story of nuclear strategy ... has been the story of intellectuals ... trying to make the atomic bomb and later the hydrogen bomb manageable, controllable, to make it conform to human proportions."[44] These thinkers have been confident that nuclear weapons can be contained and domesticated, and that, with enough cleverness, we can outmanoeuvre their menacing implications and conduct political life much as we have done in the past. They have expressed the belief that we are still able, in the nuclear age, intelligently to control the flow of events, in war as well as in peace.

It is this set of assumptions – assumptions that are central to modern military planning – that has been received with such widespread disbelief by many independent commentators who have given some thought to these matters. For it seems to many of these observers that strategies for the controlled use of nuclear weapons are unconvincing. They think that the risks involved in modern warfare are now beyond calculation. They think that, whether we like it or not, the conduct of war in the nuclear age is, in virtually all respects, completely unpredictable. As a distinguished physicist has put it, "Once nuclear war is initiated by any power, under any doctrine, in any theatre, or for any strategic or tactical purpose, the outcome will involve truly massive casualties and devastation, leading to effects on the future of mankind that are essentially uncalculable."[45] According to this view, the use of nuclear weapons, for whatever reason – whether informed by a theory of "escalation control," or perhaps pursued for the sake of coercive domination – would lead us unequivocally into the realm of the unknown and the unknowable. Such nuclear use, it is thought, would be a veritable cosmic stab in the dark, a desperate roll of the dice with apocalyptic implications.

We come, certainly, to realize how much our thinking about the nuclear age raises fundamental philosophical – perhaps even religious – questions concerning our views of human nature and of the capacity of human beings to cope with this revolutionary manifestation of power. Indeed, to a degree there has even been disagreement as to the appropriateness of the designation "revolutionary." Few people, perhaps, have rejected it entirely, but for many, especially in the armed forces and within the national security establishments, the primary concern has been to carry on with business as usual. While numerous voices have at different times drawn attention to the predicament in which we now find ourselves – as Herbert Butterfield remarked a generation ago, "we have reached the point at which our weapons have turned against us, because their destructiveness is so out of relation with any end that war can achieve for mankind"[46] – the exertions of numerous governments, especially those of the United States and the Soviet Union, have been devoted mostly to the building of more and more nuclear weapons. The tensions and contradictions that are embedded in these policies have been crisply stated by Abba Eban:

> Both the United States and the USSR accept the paradox that the main justification for possessing nuclear weapons is to deter their use; yet both nations also seek through a variety of doctrines, strategies and policies to find means of expressing their nuclear power in political terms – whether through veiled threat or the elaboration of contingency plans and scenarios in which nuclear war is treated as a concrete and viable possibility. Thus, the global imperative of preventing a nuclear holocaust collides with the exercise of sovereign power and national interest. The destiny of this planet still remains fixed on the horns of this nuclear dilemma. The nations live in an atmosphere of duality. They understand the nuclear revolution but they conduct much of their behavior as though the revolution had not occurred.[47]

These two powers have, for many years, been continually expanding and refining their nuclear arsenals. Their weaponry has become increasingly sophisticated. They have competed energetically with each other in the search for yet more awesome means of destruction. Whatever they might say in public about the horrors of nuclear war, their actions testify to a profound attraction to nuclear weapons as a vital foundation of their nations' security. Both these nations now find themselves swept up in the most extraordinary, potentially all-devouring armaments race that has ever been witnessed. And this arms race, which has implications for all nations, is very much at the centre of modern global politics, looming over all other experiences and intruding into all other matters of political importance. Understanding the dynamics of this arms race, the character of Soviet-American relations since 1945, and how we have arrived at where we now are is the primary concern of the chapter that follows.

2
Understanding the Nuclear Arms Race

1945 and Beyond

The nuclear arms race was anticipated and, in certain respects, already under way before any nuclear weapon was ever exploded. Towards the end of the Second World War, as the first fission bombs were nearing completion, some of the scientists who had helped make them began to discuss their probable impact on the future. Nazi Germany was crushed. Japan was essentially defeated, although it had not yet surrendered. And the wartime alliance with the Soviet Union was becoming, in the spring of 1945, increasingly frayed and contentious. A number of scientists in the United States, aware of the awesome new power that was about to erupt onto the world's political stage, tried to caution their political superiors. They urged restraint in the use of nuclear explosives. They thought that a surprise attack with this bomb, considering the intense secrecy that had surrounded its creation, would arouse great mistrust of American intentions. In particular, they wanted the United States to seek, as the top political priority, an agreement for the international control of nuclear power. For without such an agreement, they predicted in June of 1945, "the race for nuclear armaments will be on in earnest not later than the morning after our first demonstration of the existence of nuclear weapons. After this, it might take other nations three of four years to overcome our present head start."[1]

These predictions could hardly have been more accurate. While Soviet leaders already knew of the secret Anglo-American development of nuclear weaponry (Soviet research into nuclear power had been going on since at least 1943), the destruction of Hiroshima and Nagasaki shocked the Kremlin into urgent action. American might had been spectacularly displayed, and Soviet leaders were stunned by the dramatic state of vulnerability in which they suddenly found themselves. As David Holloway, a well-versed authority on these matters, has concluded, "while Stalin and the Soviet leaders knew of the atomic bomb before Potsdam [the site of the Big Three conference in July 1945], its significance was brought home to them only by its use in Japan. The significance was not merely that the bomb was powerful, or that it was possessed by the United States alone, but also that the United States was willing to use it in circumstances that did not seem absolutely to require it." Soviet leaders, he thinks, "regarded the use of the bomb in Japan as part of an effort to put pressure on them, as a demonstration that the United States was willing to use nuclear weapons."[2] A British journalist who was in Moscow at that time recalled that the news of the atomic bomb "had an acutely depressing effect on everybody. It was clearly realised ... that the bomb constituted a threat to Russia, and some Russian pessimists I talked to ... dismally remarked that Russia's desperately hard victory over Germany was now 'as good as wasted.'"[3] (Soviet deaths during the war, it might be recalled, had been roughly sixty-five times greater than those of the United States.)

Stalin responded to the American initiative immediately. He ordered a massive mobilization of Soviet science and industry in order to match, as quickly as possible, the American achievement. Some American military and political leaders were so disdainful of Russia and so sure of their own superiority that they confidently predicted a very long period for the u.s. nuclear monopoly. But these predictions were wrong and those of the scientists were right. In August 1949, to the shock and dismay of most Western public opinion, the Soviet Union tested its first nuclear device. The nuclear arms race had now come out of the laboratories and onto the centre of the international stage.

Under Whose Control?

Broadly conceived, the tension between the United States and the Soviet Union is neither entirely surprising nor unforeseen. Some 150

years ago, when the major decisions about global affairs were being
made mostly in London, Paris, Vienna, and, increasingly, Berlin,
Alexis de Tocqueville wrote the following words in the conclusion to
the first volume of his great work *Democracy in America* (published in
the 1830s): "There are at the present time two great nations in the
world, which started from different points, but seem to tend towards
the same end. I allude to the Russians and the Americans ... All other
nations seem to have nearly reached their natural limits, and they have
only to maintain their power; but these [two] are still in the act of
growth ... Their starting-point is different, and their courses are not the
same; yet each of them seems marked out by the will of Heaven to
sway the destinies of half the globe."[4]

De Tocqueville's prophecy has now been amply fulfilled. Both
these nations emerged from the rubble of the Second World War as the
sole, undisputed great powers. With the defeat of Germany, the Soviet
Union, though a deeply wounded society, was inevitably recognized
as the dominant power on the ravaged Eurasian continent. Continental
Europe was shattered, and Britain, while victorious in war, was
economically in decline. The United States, the only major nation that
was stronger in 1945 than it had been in 1939, was the world's
unrivalled economic power and had extensive global interests embrac-
ing both the Atlantic and the Pacific. Both nations were new to their
dominating roles. During the interwar years both had been relatively
isolated from international affairs – and from each other. As one
historian has said, they "had little in the way of common traditions, no
common political vocabulary, precious few links. They looked upon
themselves as rival models for the rest of mankind. They shared little
except distrust."[5] In the circumstances of 1945 they were, to a
substantial extent, virtually inevitable rivals, especially in Europe
(although the particular character and intensity of the rivalry was
certainly not predetermined). And into this partly predictable rivalry
was injected one completely novel and revolutionary reality: the
American atomic bomb.

The presence of this extraordinary new weapon posed problems for
American policy-makers. What, they asked, should be done with it?
What purposes might it serve? Indeed, could it be put to any good use
at all? What relevance did it have for the conduct of American foreign
policy and the search for security in a tumultuous world?

In 1945 and the succeeding several years three broad policy options were available to the United States government. First, it could actively strive to reach an agreement with other countries for the international control of nuclear energy. Such an accord, if it could be negotiated, would have one paramount purpose: it would be designed to prevent an open-ended nuclear arms race, a race that, sooner or later, would be bound to lead to a situation in which the United States would itself be vulnerable to nuclear attack from some other state. The relinquishment of one dimension of national sovereignty − state control of nuclear weapons − would, according to this view, be necessary in order to achieve any genuine long-term security. A second option opposed this position. It emphasized the advantages that could be attained from exclusive American control of the new technology. It downplayed the long-term prospects of an arms race, stressed the likelihood of decades of American nuclear superiority, and pointed to the risks of "internationalism" as against the apparently much more assured benefits of national independence and unilateral action. The proponents of this approach emphasized the need to preserve America's "atomic secret" (as it had been preserved, they thought, though mistakenly, during the Second World War) and the need to be very cautious about sharing it with foreigners. The third and final broad option took shape only towards the end of the 1940s, after the harsh antagonisms of the Cold War had imposed their icy grip on international relations. This option proposed a preventive nuclear strike against the Soviet Union. It advised that the United States consider a large-scale nuclear attack against the USSR to forestall the presumed otherwise inevitable; that is, to prevent the Soviet Union from developing its own nuclear arsenal, an arsenal that could threaten − indeed, inescapably would threaten − the fundamental security of the United States and its various allies.

We need not dwell on the various U.S.-initiated proposals for the international control of nuclear energy. For it is clear that they never had much political backing; at the highest political levels, they were not really seriously pursued. It is doubtful that President Roosevelt ever put much faith in the possibility of post-war international accords. In fact, the intense concern for secrecy that ran through the Manhattan Project was designed in part to strengthen the exclusiveness of the American mastery of nuclear energy.[6] From the spring of 1945, it is true, various voices were speaking out in favour of American concessions (those of the scientists were the most prominent), in the interest of building a foundation of trust with other nations, especially

the Soviet Union, but hard-headed politicians and military professionals were largely unmoved by their arguments. When a formal proposal
was eventually put forward for the development of mechanisms for the
international control of nuclear energy – this came to be known as the
Baruch plan, which was submitted to the United Nations in June 1946
– it was so obviously flawed, biased, and provocative (from the Soviet
point of view) that there was no chance at all that any sort of Soviet
co-operation would be forthcoming. Even close allies of the United
States were less than enthusiastic; General Andrew McNaughton,
Canada's delegate to the U.N.'s Atomic Energy Commission, later
referred to the Baruch plan as "a one-sided proposition" and
"insincerity from beginning to end."[7]

The Baruch plan included several provisions that were bound to
arouse Soviet hostility. It proposed the elimination of the Security
Council veto on matters concerning atomic energy, a veto that was of
no small importance, from Moscow's point of view, in a Western-
dominated United Nations. It proposed that severe penalties be
available against those states (such as the USSR) that were thought by
other states (such as the United States) to be violating the control plan.
In fact, this heavy emphasis on punishment and sanctions, which was a
central feature of the U.S. proposals, was hardly compatible with those
goals that, ostensibly, especially concerned American leaders: the
search for greater co-operation, trust, and international harmony. The
plan also required that the first stage of a long series of concessions
would be solely the responsibility of the Russians: the Soviet Union
was to open itself to various forms of Western scrutiny, the first of
which would be a survey and disclosure of its uranium and thorium
resources. This must have been seen by Soviet leaders as virtually a
proposal for espionage. The United States, for its part, offered no
gesture of restraint (such as a moratorium on the continuing production
and testing of atomic bombs) and proposed no initial concessions for
itself. Certainly the overall effect of the Baruch plan would have been
to place the Soviet Union in a position of long-term – perhaps
permanent – inferiority vis-a-vis the United States. Indeed, so extreme
was the American proposal, and so unaccommodating were its
demands, that it almost seems that the Baruch plan, like many
subsequent "peace" proposals from both superpowers, was designed to
be rejected. As one student of these years has concluded, "The creators
of the Baruch plan guaranteed that international control would be
entirely on American terms – or not at all."[8]

The main U.S. proposal, then, was inherently a non-starter. However, it should be emphasized that, even had it been much more attractive in its provisions, there is no assurance that the end result would have been much different. It may be that the Soviet Union, which was acutely conscious of the might of U.S. technology, felt that it had no choice but to match the American achievement and develop an independent nuclear capacity, thereby effecting (so its leaders hoped) a kind of equilibrium of international power. Without such a nuclear arsenal, the USSR risked a return to second-class status and possible overwhelming defeat in some future war. Undoubtedly the circumstances of the mid-1940s ensured that the cards were heavily stacked against the success of even the most fair-minded and even-handed proposals for international control. However, the specific terms of the Baruch plan and the smug and uncompromising spirit in which it was presented guaranteed that any glimmer of hope for internationalism that might still have existed was bound to be extinguished. The United States was not prepared to accept any of the risks that would have been involved in a serious effort to establish a framework for international co-operation. It opted instead for the risks of an arms race.

There were several pressures that strongly tilted U.S. policy away from international accords and towards exclusive control of nuclear energy. One pressure arose out of the emphasis on secrecy that had been so central to the whole history of the Manhattan Project. This preoccupation not only caused mistrust abroad of American intentions, it also encouraged many Americans to believe that there was some secret to protect, some precious formula or design plan that held the key to the making of atomic bombs, which, if "stolen" or allowed to escape, would deprive the United States of the hard-earned gains from its tremendous scientific success. This view was widely held both inside and outside government. As one historian of the immediate post-war period has observed, "Since the bombing of Hiroshima the 'atomic secret' had become an article of public as well as official faith. Stoutly defended but never understood, the idea of the secret was sacrosanct to Americans. Public-opinion surveys at the end of September 1945 revealed that some 70 per cent of the citizens and over 90 percent of the congressmen questioned objected to 'sharing the atomic-bomb secret' with other nations."[9] Any suggestions, then, that smacked of "giving away" atomic secrets came to be very unfavourably regarded, and this mood militated firmly against any effort to negotiate an agreement for the international regulation of nuclear energy.

The attitude that quickly came to prevail in the United States during the months after Hiroshima was that the atomic bomb, in the sole possession of the United States, was a "sacred trust": that the United States was the custodian of this mighty weapon in the interests of all mankind. The notion of sharing control with other nations, which was certainly widely discussed, came to be regarded by many Americans as uncongenial (the increasing tension in u.s.-Soviet relations, largely rooted in Europe, contributed to these sentiments); and, as public discussions and debates continued, opinion gradually moved away from a sympathetic regard for international co-operation and towards support for monopoly control. Of course, this increasing attachment to exclusive possession implied an acceptance of the inevitability of an armaments race. And the acceptance of this prospect was made easier to bear because of the fairly widespread opinion, which was actively fostered by a number of prominent political and military leaders, that "we could stay ahead," that, with vigilance and firmness of purpose, the u.s. nuclear predominance could be maintained far into the future.

This confidence in the likely longevity of American superiority was rooted very much in a particular view of the Soviet Union and its capabilities. It was widely suggested (though not by most competent scientists) that the Russians would be slow to develop their own bomb (a few even wondered if they would ever do so). This belief, when it was encouraged by public officials, was founded largely on two claims: first, that there was no or little suitable uranium in the Soviet Union, and thus the USSR would be lacking the key resource for nuclear fission; and second, that for a very long time the Soviet Union would lack the sort of vital know-how – the industrial base, the engineering skills, the advanced technology – which would be essential for any conceivable Russian version of the Manhattan Project. Given these deficiencies, it was argued, the Soviet Union was not likely to be much of a nuclear rival. Americans could thus look forward to many more years of security. And if long-term security was such a good bet, then it was not clear that there was any pressing need for inordinate co-operation with foreigners or for "giving up" what was already possessed. In such a political climate the fragile ideal of internationalism could hardly hope to attract much of a following.

Increasingly, in u.s. political and military circles, what was actually being envisaged was the exact opposite of international controls. The ideal future that was taking shape – at least in many official imaginations – was that of an American-administered Pax Atomica. According to this influential view, an American monopoly of atomic bombs would better allow the United States to function as a global peacekeeper and to ensure more effectively that its own agenda for world peace and order was accepted, or at least properly respected, by other nations. As some of them were to express it, the bomb was their "winning weapon," not necessarily in military terms, but certainly diplomatically. The bomb was seen as a major bargaining tool. It would help to concentrate the minds of other states on the merits of u.s. policy objectives. In short, the anticipated long-enduring monopoly of nuclear weapons would help effect the construction of a robust and dynamic new world order, with the United States itself as its leading architect.[10]

Air-Atomic Strategy

The dominant themes of American nuclear policy did not, of course, emerge fully developed with the end of the Second World War. Initially, in fact, there was much confusion and uncertainty, and many competing opinions were circulating in Washington. One could hardly expect that the full implications of such an extraordinary weapon would be rapidly and clearly comprehended. For many months there was no general agreement as to what to do, strategically and politically, with the new technology. Some thought that everything had changed, others that little had changed. Was a fundamental rethinking of military policy now essential? If so, in what direction should this rethinking proceed? The fluid and uncommitted state of official thinking at this time is suggested by, among other things, the very small number of bombs that existed in the American arsenal: two in late 1945, nine in 1946, thirteen in 1947.[11] It was only from around 1948 that American policy became explicitly, overtly, and self-consciously committed to a particular view of nuclear weapons – a view that was shaped by both the recent experiences of total war and the newer realities of the Cold War.

American policy, as it took shape in the later 1940s, was in many respects largely an extension of the practice of so-called strategic bombing that had been so enthusiastically adopted by the Anglo-American air forces during the Second World War. The recent war had witnessed the triumph of a doctrine that championed the centrality of airpower, an airpower that could penetrate behind enemy lines and deliver devastating attacks against the cities and industrial infrastructure of the other side. In this way, it was claimed, civilian morale would be undermined and the enemy's ability to sustain its military machine would be severely crippled. (It was learned, after the war, that these objectives of strategic bombing had been largely unfulfilled, a failure that was not highly publicized, especially by air forces.) These precedents from the previous war of area bombing seemed especially relevant to the circumstances of the nuclear age, at least in the eyes of the air force and its supporters. For surely, they thought, the atomic bomb would serve admirably to make airpower – in which America was already overwhelmingly supreme – that much more effective and awe-inspiring. The presence of the bomb, it was felt, would permit its American possessor to deal more convincingly with "aggressors," and perhaps as well with those states that might be disposed to challenge the post-war world order, as the United States wanted to see it created.

This emphasis on air-atomic strategy, as a coherent policy, became especially pronounced after 1947. Increasingly, the Soviet Union was being seen as the principal adversary of the United States. Its intentions were thought to be deeply hostile; its policies resolutely expansionist; its goals fundamentally incompatible with the liberal, capitalist internationalism of the United States. If Soviet aggression were to be resisted, it came to be believed that appropriate constraints could be imposed only by virtue of the power of the atomic bomb. The bomb, many thought, was the only credible counterweight that the United States could pose to the might of Soviet land forces, notably the strength of the Red Army in eastern and central Europe. The core of this case was bluntly stated by H.H. Arnold, an influential air force general who was one of the keenest advocates of the centrality of airpower: "Russia has no fear of an army; she thinks hers is just as good as, and bigger than, any in the world; she has no fear of a navy, since she cannot see how it can be employed against her; but she does fear our long-range Strategic Air Force, which she cannot as yet match, or as yet understand. In the Strategic Air Force, coupled with our atomic bomb ... we hold the balance of power in the world."[12]

The atomic bomb, then, was allotted an increasingly prominent role in American defence planning. It came to be regarded as a deterrent against a wide range of possible Soviet actions – actions that American policy-makers might construe as hostile, or unacceptable, or threatening to certain vital national interests. In this emerging strategy atomic weapons were seen clearly as means to fight and win wars, if necessary. The terror they engendered was regarded as salutary. And as Soviet-American relations deteriorated, especially following the Communist coup in Czechoslovakia in February 1948 and the Berlin blockade shortly thereafter, whatever doubts there had been about the military utility of nuclear weapons – doubts concerning the feasibility of actually using them to achieve particular political ends – greatly receded, and in some official circles they were completely abandoned. By the end of the decade the bomb had come to be, in many respects, the centre-piece of American defence policy.

This self-conscious *nuclearization* of American military policy was a momentous development. It testified to the confidence that u.s. leaders placed in weapons of mass destruction. It expressed their faith in the political utility of these weapons, the leverage that possession of them afforded. For many of these men the bomb was a decisive factor in the conduct of Cold War diplomacy. Rather than evincing caution and public restraint in the face of nuclear weapons and a recognition of their "uniqueness" and fearful power, American policy-makers tended to think in terms of their usability and the messages of strength they would convey to Moscow. Just as the dollar was to become the principal medium of international economic exchange, so too the bomb would be established as the predominant currency of great power politics. This was very much a u.s.-drafted agenda and one that conditioned much of the tone and many of the priorities of world politics in subsequent years. At the centre of this agenda, as Americans saw it, was a nuclear-based security policy. As one prominent Senator put it in July 1949, "the concept of strategic bombardment with atomic weapons in case of war … is the keystone of our military policy and a foundation pillar of our foreign policy as well."[13] Nuclear weapons had, in short order, been elevated to pride of place in the defence posture of the nation.

As this strategy became more explicit, the nuclear arsenal rapidly expanded. There were thirteen bombs in 1947, fifty in 1948, and around 300 in 1950; by 1953 the stockpile had grown to an estimated 1,000 nuclear bombs.[14] (The Soviet Union still had very few usable bombs and none that could be delivered against the United States.) By the early 1950s nuclear bombs were being mass produced and fully integrated into the operational planning of the American armed forces.

Dependence on them grew; they became, in many respects, the mainstay of the "Free World's" defence. From 1953 they were made available to NATO forces in Europe, thereby initiating the process that would result in the subsequent heavy nuclearization of European defence strategy, with all its attendant problems for a later generation. As East-West tensions increased and as Soviet military technology gained ground (as it was bound to), the United States became even more determined to pursue the arms race with vigour and to work energetically to stay ahead of its Soviet competitor. As Lawrence Freedman has observed, "The response in the U.S. to the evidence of a developing Soviet capability for both the manufacture and delivery of atom bombs was not to back down from reliance on nuclear weapons but to raise the stakes, moving to the development of hydrogen bombs, so ushering in an age of nuclear plenty and confirming a trend towards ever-increasing levels of destruction."[15]

The nuclear ante, which had already been growing, was raised substantially from the early 1950s. In January 1950 President Truman approved the development of the hydrogen bomb, and in November 1952 the United States tested its first thermonuclear device. The logical outcome of the increase in nuclear dependence was the doctrine, enunciated early in the Eisenhower administration, of "massive retaliation": the declared threat by the United States to respond to what it saw as Communist aggression, at any time and in any place, with devastating force, including, if it so decided, nuclear force. The might of the U.S. nuclear arsenal was repeatedly stressed, sometimes explicitly, more frequently implicitly. As one student of these years has observed, "The unmistakable message of this rhetoric was that the administration had made the threat of retaliation with nuclear weapons against an enemy's homeland the cornerstone of its national security policy."[16] High officials were quite explicit, at least in certain forums, in clarifying the thrust of American policy. Admiral Arthur Radford, chairman of the Joint Chiefs of Staff, stated the official position unequivocally in a confidential speech that he delivered to the Naval War College in Newport, Rhode Island, in May 1954. "Atomic forces," he stated, "are now our primary forces." "Actions by other forces, on land, sea or air are relegated to a secondary role." This meant, he observed, "that nuclear weapons, fission and fusion, will be used in the next major war. Availability of fissile material, the economy of its use, the magnitude of its destructive effects, and the flexibility of its use makes it the primary munition of war. Victory will come to the side that makes the best use of it."[17]

It is clear that the nuclear threat, in response to the perceived Soviet menace, came to dominate profoundly the American search for national security. This threat seemed to give the United States a major initiative in its global struggle against Communism. It seemed to put real bite into the policy of containment, a policy that many Republicans, so long out of power, had come to regard as toothless, timid, and dangerously reactive. It seemed to confront the Kremlin at that point where the Soviets were weak and vulnerable. The national security policy of the Republican administration, it has been said, "flowed from the strong belief of the president and his top policy advisers in the utility of nuclear weapons for both deterrent and actual military missions."[18] Nuclear strength, it was firmly believed, could be readily converted into political advantage. On several occasions during these years the United States threatened to use nuclear weapons, when it felt that such threats would persuade a foe of its resolve and seriousness. And it also indicated a willingness, "if necessary," to follow through on these threats. As John Gaddis has pointed out, "It is clear, in retrospect, that the Eisenhower administration was prepared to 'go nuclear' in any of several contingencies – a Soviet conventional force attack in Europe, a violation of the Korean armistice, a decision to intervene directly in Indochina, or a Chinese Communist assault on Quemoy and Matsu."[19] These were threats that had to be taken seriously in foreign capitals; for at this time the United States was the only nation in a position to so brandish its nuclear weapons. One would imagine that its willingness to act in this manner must have stiffened the resolve in the Kremlin to "neutralize" the u.s. nuclear arsenal, or, perhaps, even to turn the table on its capitalist adversary.

The concern during the 1950s to highlight the role of nuclear weapons was accompanied by a determination to play down the differences between these new weapons and conventional armaments. The distinctions between them were blurred. It was often suggested and sometimes openly stated that there was no real difference between the use of nuclear and non-nuclear weapons. Nuclear weapons, it was said, should be seen as military tools much like other tools in the arsenal. As John Foster Dulles, the secretary of state, explained to a closed NATO ministerial meeting in April 1954, the United States believed that nuclear weapons "must now be treated as in fact having become 'conventional.'" "It should be our agreed policy," he said, "in case of war, to use atomic weapons as conventional weapons against the military assets of the enemy whenever and wherever it would be of advantage to do so."[20]

During these years, when the United States had an overwhelming nuclear superiority, it was promoting a kind of normalizing of the status of these weapons. It was according them a sense of the commonplace; it was suggesting that to use them would not be all that remarkable. Given the conscious adoption of a policy of marked nuclear dependence, such talk, perhaps, was unavoidable, a necessary way of justifying what had been decided on for other reasons. But such talk was not cost-free. As Bernard Brodie pointed out a few years later, at the end of the 1950s: "although a considerable residue of anathema and horror for the use of nuclear weapons remains in the world today, it has been considerably eroded by repeated insistence, emanating mostly from the United States, that the use of nuclear weapons must be regarded as absolutely normal, natural, and right. Whether it was really in the American interest to attack the emotional resistances to using nuclear weapons was never soberly examined."[21] (One should recall this evidence from a generation ago when it is alleged today, as it often is, that Soviet leaders lack a proper respect for the special horrors of nuclear weapons. Indeed, as we shall notice later, this allegedly less humane Soviet attitude is now presented as a major component of the official American image of the "Soviet threat.")

Two further points may be made about the ascendancy of this nuclear-dominated policy. First, its attractiveness derived very much from its relative cheapness and its immediate popular appeal. Any alternative policy would have had to put much more stress on conventional forces, and these forces would have cost more (more troops, larger quantities of weapons) and probably would have necessitated some sort of broadly based, if not universal, military training. Fiscal conservatism, then, and public dislike of anything that resembled conscription, were allies of the proponents of air-atomic power. As Michael Howard has observed, "Governments, and the majorities on which they relied, found in nuclear weapons so convenient a solution to their budgetary problems that they were adopted almost without question."[22] Nuclear bombs saved money and manpower. They allowed the United States to play from strength, the strength and dynamism of its sophisticated technology, as against the labour-intensive Red Army. The confidence placed in nuclear bombs was reflected in the rapid and substantial military demobilization that occurred at the end of the war, from some 12 million to 1.7 million troops in the United States (the USSR demobilized too, though not to the same extent: there were around 3 million men in the Soviet armed forces in early 1948, down from almost 12 million in 1945). The triumph of air-atomic power, then, was partly a consequence of the wholesale reduction of non-nuclear military force.

My second point relates to the short-term thinking that informed this nuclear-based policy. Its benefits, such as they were, could last only as long as the USSR was nuclear-weak. Most people, one would have thought, could have recognized that this was bound to be a temporary state of affairs. But it seems that the longer-term implications of depending so heavily on weapons of mass destruction did not cause much politically significant loss of sleep. And yet this was a policy that was based, first, on the assumption of a long-lived American monopoly of nuclear weapons; and secondly, when this monopoly was ended, on the assumption of a continuing and sustained U.S. technological superiority over the Soviet Union. The widespread feeling was that the United States could stay ahead. Indeed, if one side of the coin of U.S. international attitudes was a kind of paranoia and morbid pessimism in the face of Communism, the other side was a robust confidence in the superiority of all things American, especially the potency of American enterprise and technology. Had the implausibility of these assumptions about long-term Russian inferiority and weakness been more widely noticed, U.S. nuclear dependence – indeed, the actual striving to impose an American Pax Atomica – might not have gone as far as it did. As General Maxwell Taylor, army chief of staff between 1955 and 1959 and one of the critics of this dependence, later put it, "this reliance on Massive Retaliation overlooked the fact that atomic bangs could eventually be bought for rubles as well as dollars."[23] Once the Soviet Union demonstrated that it, too, could produce nuclear weapons in abundance, the fragility of American strategy, in particular the highly militarized sense of containment and the concept of "extended" nuclear deterrence, was cruelly exposed, at least for those who cared to see. The USSR came to be able to do to the United States what the United States had been able to do to it. And in these circumstances, which came about in the

1960s, the credibility of the nuclear threat, as applied to a wide range of political conflicts, was very much called into question. When massive destruction could be mutually rendered, more minds were turned to thinking about other routes to national security, such as arms limitations. But whatever doctrine was dominant at a given moment, whether the stress was on massive retaliation or limited nuclear war or flexible response, there was a persistent commitment to the notion that nuclear weapons could be made into useful tools in the conduct of foreign policy.

Meanwhile, the nuclear arsenals kept growing. When Eisenhower was elected, there were around 1,000 warheads in the u.s. nuclear stockpile; by the time he left office the arsenal totalled some 20,000 warheads.[24] New delivery systems were also being developed. In fact, the technology of mass destruction advanced so rapidly that strategy, rather than leading, was almost always being led. Few wondered very long or very loudly about the point of it all.

Preventive War

While there are many things in the nuclear age that might have happened but did not happen, one of these non-occurrences deserves some comment. The United States, during the decade after Hiroshima, did not launch a preventive nuclear attack against the Soviet Union, even though some people both then and later felt that it could have done so, with excellent prospects of success. Given the failure to reach any agreement concerning the international control of nuclear power, this was the only way that the bomb could have been kept out of Soviet hands – or, at least from 1949, prevented from becoming an arsenal of bombs. The notion of a preventive first-strike was based on the assumption that a military show-down with Russia was inevitable. The conflict between them was thought to be so fundamental that it was bound to lead sooner or later to war. If this were so, then surely the most sensible course of action was to destroy Russia before it had a chance fully to mobilize its resources and get its own stockpile of weapons of mass destruction.

It is not yet entirely clear how seriously these ideas were taken. What we can say is that there was a fair amount of discussion of the notion, both openly and privately, and that it enjoyed some currency in influential political and military circles. From the Soviet point of view, as one authority has said, "There was certainly enough preventive war talk in the United States to suggest that the danger of such a war could not be entirely excluded."[25] (Subsequent Soviet writing on these years has not failed to notice the various threatening statements that were forthcoming from a number of prominent Americans.)[26] Some American military officers advocated a preventive war, and a few senators found the idea appealing and wondered about its feasibility.[27] Exasperation with the course of u.s.-Soviet relations after 1947 sometimes gave rise to tough talk. Walter Lippmann, the powerful journalist and political insider, heard some of this talk in the early spring of 1948, shortly after the coup in Czechoslovakia. The secretary of defense, James Forrestal, "suggested to Lippmann over lunch that the United States might have to launch a preventive war against the Soviet Union. Air Force Secretary Stuart Symington echoed his boss's sentiments a few days later when he told Lippmann that unless the Russians agreed to pull out of Eastern Europe and open their bases to American inspection, the air force should knock out their key cities with atomic bombs."[28] Such thoughts were still very much alive during the first year or so of the Eisenhower administration. According to one student of u.s. nuclear policy, "Although seldom explicitly discussed in writing, preventive war was implicit in some of the major policy deliberations of the time" (i.e., in 1953–4).[29] Nor were such suggestions confined exclusively to generals, right-wing politicians, and Russophobe intellectuals. The idea of a preventive nuclear attack was also sympathetically mentioned by, among others, Bertrand Russell, who argued that Russia should be threatened with such an attack in order to force it to agree to the sort of international controls and programs for nuclear disarmament that were incorporated in the Baruch plan.[30]

In trying to understand why these suggestions were never implemented, or, indeed, why they were only occasionally taken seriously at the highest levels of government, one has to acknowledge the importance of moral and ideological restraints. There were no precedents in the American political past that would justify a completely unprovoked attack. Such an attack would be contrary to American ideals. It would be widely regarded as an expression of naked imperialism, an attempt to achieve world order by conquest. It would involve the slaughter of millions of innocent civilians and physical devastation totally without parallel. American democracy itself might be jeopardized as a result of such a flagrantly militaristic initiative. Public opinion would certainly be, to say the least, vastly aroused, and mistrust of the United States in other countries would be acute. A writer who had served as a U.S. diplomat during these years has put this argument in the following way: "If the Government in Washington had undertaken to use the atomic bomb to control the world it would surely have ended by incurring the fanatical hostility of the world's peoples, with incalculable consequences. It would have found itself trying to dominate the world by terror alone; it would have found itself driven to ever greater extremes of ruthlessness; and the requirements of a totally ruthless policy would, at last, have compelled it to establish a tyranny over the American people as well as over the rest of mankind."[31]

This sort of thinking was important. But also important was the probability that a preventive attack would not work, militarily and politically. There were a number of reasons for scepticism. First, even in narrow military terms, success was by no means assured. Because of the American monopoly of air-atomic power, the USSR had invested heavily in air defences, and a lot of the slow-moving bombers of that day might well have been shot down. Moreover, the United States was lacking in certain critical technical resources, such as reliable maps of many parts of the Soviet Union. The cities in European Russia undoubtedly could have been largely destroyed, but the industrial centres further east would have been much less vulnerable. Second, and of greater importance, while the Soviet Union would have been unable to respond with nuclear weapons against an American nuclear attack, it certainly could have retaliated by invading parts of western Europe. Such an invasion could not have been stopped with American conventional forces, and the use of nuclear bombs against Soviet troops that might occupy, say, Hamburg, Munich, Frankfurt, and the like was unlikely to win many friends. Western Europe, then, was something of a hostage; by threatening it, Russia could counter American nuclear supremacy. The expansion of the Red Army from 1948, after the very substantial post-war Soviet demobilization, was probably designed partly with this retaliatory option in mind. Third, it was by no means clear that a nuclear attack against Russia, even if it succeeded in certain military terms, could be at all politically conclusive. It was not likely to result in a "permanent solution." It was not clear that a Soviet recovery could be prevented; perhaps another

Russia would, in time, emerge from the ashes and again challenge u.s. hegemony. It was feared, in other words, that even if a sort of victory might be achieved, it would be a politically hollow victory, a victory that would give no assurance of long-term international security and stability.[32]

Many considerations deterred the United States from following the theoretical path of preventive war. As a way of saving the world, it was too politically crude, too much a huge leap in the dark, too likely to backfire, too morally repellant. Even as the bomb was becoming the mainstay of American "strength," it was much easier to argue its virtues in the abstract, and in general terms, than it was to contemplate in detail and with political realism its actual use to snuff out the threat of Communism.

Arms Racing

As one reviews the conduct of East-West relations since 1945 and the early history of the nuclear age, one soon comes to recognize one of the central components of the nuclear arms race between the United States and the Soviet Union: its *reciprocality*. New weapons on one side call forth new weapons from the other side. What one superpower is doing during any particular time is intelligible only in the light of what the other superpower has already done, or has started to do, or is expected to do. One side acts (or seems to be acting or is expected to act), the other side reacts – perhaps even "overreacts" – and takes steps which, in turn, prompt new actions from the other side. The post-war American monopoly of nuclear bombs was regarded by Soviet leaders as dangerous and intolerable (the British, apparently, were also alarmed),[33] and they resolved to get their own bombs as quickly as possible. The Soviet nuclear test in August 1949 exacerbated American feelings of insecurity and contributed to the presidential decision a few months later to develop the hydrogen "superbomb." These American developments in turn stimulated Soviet thermo-nuclear research and development.[34] The u.s. nuclear stockpile was by this time growing very rapidly, war in Korea broke out in June 1950, and, with the rise of McCarthyism, the Cold War entered its most frigid and fanatical phase. With the formal espousal of the doctrine of massive retaliation in 1953–4, the centrality of nuclear weapons in the conduct of u.s. foreign policy and the strikingly militarized concept of East-West relations that held sway in Washington were made manifest for all to see.

Both superpowers, having launched themselves unequivocally into an open-ended arms race, worked actively through the 1950s to improve their explosive devices and the means of delivering them. The appearance of the first Sputnik in 1957 triggered much fear in the United States that the Soviet Union was forging ahead. There was widespread talk of a dangerous "missile gap," and vigorous measures were taken under both Eisenhower and Kennedy to develop a substantial arsenal of nuclear missiles, some of which were based on land, others in submarines. In fact, the alleged missile gap, as insiders knew in 1960, was non-existent. But this misperception could not be easily corrected politically. The new American missiles were deployed, and the result, by 1962, was that the United States had a commanding nuclear missile superiority over the Soviet Union. In late 1961 the USSR had only a handful of operational intercontinental missiles – almost certainly less than ten. Contrary to many of the previous predictions, it was the Soviet Union, not the United States, that became dramatically vulnerable. American military planners were not unaware of the advantages they had come to enjoy. As Fred Kaplan has observed: "With so few Soviet missiles – that is, so few counterforce targets – a successful attack would require far fewer American weapons and could tolerate much less thorough and precise coordination. In the first major crisis that faced the Kennedy Administration [Berlin in 1961], several high-ranking officials in the Pentagon and the White House viewed a disarming, damage-limiting counterforce strike as an attractive option indeed."[35] All this could hardly have sat well with Moscow. Indeed, no less a figure than Robert McNamara, President Kennedy's secretary of defense, has made just this point. By 1962, he recalls, "the advantage in the U.S. warhead inventory was so great vis-a-vis the Soviets that the Air Force was saying that they felt we had a first-strike capability and could, and should, continue to have one. If the Air Force thought that, imagine what the Soviets thought. And assuming they thought that, how would you expect them to react? The way they reacted was by substantially expanding their strategic nuclear weapons programme."[36]

In response, then, to the American missile buildup of the early 1960s, the USSR launched a massive buildup of its own, which became especially pronounced after the ousting from power of Nikita

Khrushchev in 1964. From the mid-1960s the Soviet Union deployed hundreds of new missiles. While the United States did not respond fully in kind, partly because it was already so far ahead, partly because of the morass in which it found itself in Vietnam, it did decide to deploy MIRVs (multiple independently targetable re-entry vehicles), an innovation that greatly increased the destructive capacities of its existing and on-stream missiles. The Soviet Union, as usual, later emulated this American breakthrough, with the result that by the late 1970s the meaningful destructive capacities of both nuclear arsenals were roughly equivalent – equivalent at levels that would have seemed incredible only a generation before. The United States, in short, had come to experience the same vulnerability to devastating attack that Russia had been living with for three decades.

We have now entered another phase of this extraordinary rivalry. The Soviet buildup is being countered by the United States, with new and more accurate land- and submarine-based missiles, with a new long-range bomber, with "stealth" radar-resistant air-technology, and with several thousand cruise missiles. Each superpower seems (at least to the other side) to be deploying weapons that are designed to degrade the other's retaliatory capabilities. Each fears that the other is pursuing a counterforce edge, that is, a superior capacity to knock out the nuclear assets – missiles, bombers, control centres, and the like – of its rival. Each is thus racing hard to try to prevent this from happening. If the present very ambitious American arms buildup proceeds apace, as now seems likely, it is certain that the Soviet Union will respond with new offensive weapons of its own later in this decade and into the 1990s.

The two superpowers have become locked together in a rivalry to which there is no end in view. And as this arms race proceeds, with each side constantly speaking of the need to "strengthen its deterrent," national security for both, rather than being in any way enhanced, is continuously eroded.

Nuclear Superiority

For most of the post-war period the leading edge of the nuclear arms race has been pushed forward by the United States. The major technological innovations have been mostly American-made. It is American military doctrine that, since shortly after Hiroshima, has stressed the utility of nuclear weapons and a willingness to use them. For a number of years American leaders publicly emphasized the overwhelming nuclear superiority of their nation. Even when the subsequent expansion of the Soviet arsenal raised doubts about the merits of u.s. military priorities (especially the emphasis on massive retaliation), the desirability of keeping the nuclear lead and preserving some sort of clear-cut predominance was widely endorsed and promoted in official circles. For the sake of safety, most people thought, the United States should always be striving to stay at least a few steps ahead. As one authority wrote in 1975, "Nuclear superiority over the Soviet Union has been a major political goal of American defense planners in the postwar period."[37] Desmond Ball, an expert commentator on the arms competition, concurs with this judgment: "Throughout both the Eisenhower Administration of the 1950s and the Kennedy and Johnson Administrations of the 1960s, an enduring guiding principle governing the size of u.s. strategic nuclear forces was that of *superiority* over the Soviet Union. This was an assumption fundamental to the thinking of military and civilian strategists and politicians alike, with few exceptions." "Regardless," he says, "of the various nuances of u.s. nuclear strategy during the years in which the Kennedy-McNamara buildup was programmed," – and diverse views were espoused – "the determination of the Pentagon to ensure strategic superiority was constant."[38]

Exactly what superiority meant, and how to identify it, were not always easy to establish, especially after the mid-1960s, when Soviet missiles came into their own. But before this massive Soviet buildup occurred, maintaining an imposing nuclear advantage seemed to many military men both feasible and self-evidently desirable. General Thomas S. Power, commander in chief of Strategic Air Command between 1957 and 1964, offered the following opinion on the character of the nuclear arms competition: "no race is ever decided until the goal line is reached, and neither we nor the Soviets have reached it – assured peace in a Free World for us and world domination for the Soviets. If we should ever slacken our pace in the belief that no one can win the race anyway because of the mythical nuclear stalement, we would make it easy for the Soviets to catch up with us and surpass us all along the line. However, if we keep on forging ahead, gauging our pace by that of the Soviets, we can always stay ahead of them sufficiently to protect our 'deterrent margin.'"[39] As Curtis LeMay, chief of staff of the u.s. air force between 1961 and 1965, put it in 1965, "At the present time we hold an overwhelming advantage. But if we loll around and do nothing, we won't have the advantage for long. We must keep that overwhelming superiority." To him the notion that a kind of nuclear stalemate (i.e., mutual deterrence) was emerging, and whose emergence could not be prevented, was clearly anathema.[40]

To many in the u.s. defence establishment the notions of nuclear parity and mutual deterrence were completely unacceptable. They rejected the implicit restraints that such thinking imposed. This resistance was particularly pronounced in the u.s. air force and among its supporters. "For them," as General Maxwell Taylor pointed out, "the growth of the Soviet nuclear power changed nothing in the situation other than to accentuate the need for more atomic weapons and more delivery vehicles to stay safely ahead of the Russians."[41] And part of the point of staying ahead, as Robert McNamara has recalled, was to ensure a first-strike capability, that is, the ability to initiate a nuclear war with the ussr and to emerge victorious. "Many Air Force generals were quite explicit about their desire for such a posture," according to Desmond Ball.[42] General Thomas Power thought that "it would be a grave mistake to give the Soviets the impression that we would never strike first."[43] "A war fought from ... a base of nuclear superiority," argued General LeMay in 1968, "would leave the United States sorely wounded, but viable and victorious." A strategy of this sort, he acknowledged, "would suggest the capability of a first strike – of initiating nuclear war. Such a suggestion is absolutely necessary if the United States is to prevail in the diplomatic world." Deterrence, he asserted, "cannot be achieved with a second-strike facade. Conceding the enemy the first blow simply invites him to find a way to smother our retaliation." Deterrence "must rest not only upon the ability to withstand a first strike and retaliate effectively, but on the ability to launch a first strike and win if necessary." He was still firmly of the view – and this view had been shared by many others – that "our general war strategy should be designed to prevail and defeat the enemy under a variety of circumstances, and not to rule out a first strike."[44] (This kind of thinking, which fell somewhat out of fashion after the early 1960s, has enjoyed a revival since the late 1970s.)

Because of the intense secrecy that hangs over all deliberations in the Kremlin, we know little in detail about Soviet views of these American actions and policy declarations. Certainly the Soviet leadership was given good grounds for fearing what, in its own eyes, might have been seen as a kind of American nuclear adventurism. One writer thinks that "Massive retaliation was perceived by Kremlin leaders as a provocative policy that suggested the specter of a u.s. first strike and raised the very real possibility of nuclear blackmail by American leaders. These fears," he suggests, "contributed to Khrushchev's rocket rattling strategy and the high level of tension between Washington and Moscow."[45] (Khrushchev's boastful blustering was partly intended to conceal the real weaknesses in the Soviet defence posture. In this he was all too successful.) The American nuclear threat, which was certainly taken seriously in Moscow, was soon reciprocated in kind, to evident Soviet satisfaction, with the arrival of intercontinental missiles (Soviet bombers were unable to reach the American heartland and return to base). "Only by building up a nuclear missile force," writes Nikita Khrushchev in his memoirs, "could we keep the enemy from unleashing war against us." He proceeds to offer his version of Sputnik and the other significant military developments of his years in power: "if we had given the West a chance, war would have been declared while Dulles was alive. But we were the first to launch rockets into space; we exploded the most powerful nuclear devices; we accomplished those feats first, ahead of the United States, England, and France. Our accomplishments and our obvious might had a sobering effect on the aggressive forces in the [West] ... They knew that they had lost their chance to strike at us with impunity."[46] "Of course," he admitted, "we tried to derive maximum political advantage from the fact that we were the first to launch our rockets into space. We wanted to exert pressure on American militarists – and also influence the minds of more reasonable politicians – so that the United States would start treating us better."[47] The immediate American reaction – aside from consternation – was to build even more missiles than it had originally planned to build.

It is clear that, during these years, and probably more recently as well, Soviet decisions have been made in no small degree in response to the actions of the United States. This, in part, was how Khrushchev justified his attempt to install missiles in Cuba in 1962. "In addition to protecting Cuba," he claimed (the notion here was that missiles in Cuba would deter another effort by the United States to invade that socialist country), "our missiles would have equalized what the West likes to call 'the balance of power.' The Americans had surrounded our country with military bases and threatened us with nuclear weapons, and now they would learn just what it feels like to have enemy missiles pointing at you; we'd be doing nothing more than giving them a little of their own medicine. And it was high time America learned what it feels like to have her own land and her own people threatened."[48] It is likely that at many other times Soviet actions have been vitally shaped by American policies. As the Israeli diplomat Abba Eban has observed, "Many stages of progress in the Soviet military build-up have been reactive; they have been direct consequences of United States initiatives." The Soviets themselves have only occasionally set the pace in the arms race (as in 1957–8). But they have displayed an unequivocal determination to match, at least very broadly, whatever the Americans do, strategically speaking. And this determination is an integral and persistent component of their foreign policy. Abba Eban has clearly identified this major Soviet objective:

> The central aim of its diplomacy is to secure worldwide recognition of its status as one of the two superpowers, with a capacity equal to that of the United States to impress itself on the international order ... Moscow is not prepared to be a regional power centered on Europe while the United States alone wields global responsibilities. The most deep-seated yearning of the Soviet Union is to be regarded as America's equal in the world power balance. The pursuit of a strong nuclear posture was inspired by a passion for status as well as by military considerations.[49]

The United States, having for so long defined great power status – at least very substantially – in terms of the possession of weapons of mass destruction, set an example that others have made haste to follow.

Reciprocalities of Fear

The ongoing arms race between the two superpowers has been and still is fuelled by mutual fears and distrust. Each superpower has been, at different times and to varying degrees, acutely anxious for its own security. Fear has been aroused in each nation by the power of the other; each has feared the other's intentions and imagined the worst. Soviet fears have tended to focus on Western technological superiority, the security of Russia's far-flung borders, and the possibility of hostile encirclement. Indeed, a deep sort of insecurity has loomed persistently over Russian experience in a manner unknown to the histories of, say, England, Canada, or the United States. Fear of foreigners – foreign cultural influences, foreign economic dynamism, invasion by foreigners – has been of critical importance in the Russian experience of nationhood. These fears have not diminished since the Bolshevik revolution or since the Soviet triumph over Nazi Germany. After 1945, as a thoughtful Australian diplomat has pointed out, Soviet leaders "were not without reasons for fear: America did encircle Russia by a chain of bases and did utter threats about 'the massive retaliation' of thermo-nuclear war and did re-arm Germany and did favour Japan, and the American press, and not a few American politicians, did threaten Russia repeatedly."[50] With the revival from the late 1970s in the United States of harsh anti-Soviet declamations, Soviet anxieties concerning their nation's security apparently intensified – along with, it should be said, a growing disposition to act defiantly in the face of what the Kremlin saw as American "provocation."[51]

American fears, which are much more recent and much more historically unaccustomed – the American mainland, after all, has never been invaded – have tended to focus on the numerical superiority of Soviet land forces, the risk of surprise attack, and the erosion of American influence in unstable regions of the world. Geopolitical realities have ensured that, if Russians fear encirclement, Americans fear that the USSR, as the most important power in the world's "heartland" (i.e., the Eurasian continent), will be tempted to expand into those regions that are on or near its borders (western Europe, the Middle East), thereby isolating the United States in its own, considerably smaller, hemisphere, and depriving it of access to a truly world-wide economy. Americans also entertain frequent anxieties as to a devastating first-strike against their territory, a kind of repeat of the nightmare of Pearl Harbor. Moreover, these particular fears have not been eased by certain actual changes in global power relations that have occurred since the Second World War. In 1945 and shortly thereafter the vitality and robust self-confidence of the United States were, in part, a consequence of the weaknesses of all other states. This overwhelming predominance came to be seen by many Americans as normal and natural – even as a kind of manifest destiny. But other nations, including the Soviet Union, were sure to rebuild their strength. And as a consequence of this rebuilding, the relative superiority of the United States was bound to erode, a process to which many Americans, perhaps understandably, have not been easily reconciled. In the 1980s one has noticed considerable nostalgia for these earlier and, in many eyes, simpler years. This nostalgia finds it hard to accept some of the present realities of world politics: realities that include revolutionary upheaval in many Third World countries, the loss of u.s. nuclear hegemony, and a situation of totally unprecedented American vulnerability to enemy attack.

Both superpowers have justified their actions, to both themselves and the world, in terms of self-defence. Each has seen itself as acting strictly in the interests of its own security. As John Gaddis has remarked, "Both the Soviet Union and the United States have explained their projection of influence over much of the rest of the world as necessary to protect themselves against the other."[52] At the end of the Second World War, each nation found itself in vastly different circumstances from those that had prevailed only a few years before, and each was concerned to make its own future more secure – in its own way. Looking back on this post-war period, Louis Halle, a diplomat at that time, recalls that "Neither Moscow nor Washington was aiming to conquer the world. But the abrupt and largely unpremeditated expansion of Russian power at the end of the War had provoked the defensive expansion of American power, which had provoked a similar Russian reaction. As in the Punic Wars, both sides were moved primarily by defensive considerations, and both sides suspected or at least accused the other of wishing to conquer the world."[53] (The proposition that Moscow is bent on world conquest is, of course, still widely and uncritically accepted, especially in the United States.)

Each superpower has certainly seen the international arena from very different perspectives. For the United States, its national self-interest has been largely compatible with the preservation of the political status quo. (It is American technology and commerce that have been revolutionary.) The Soviet Union, on the other hand, though hardly a revolutionary power in the conduct of its policy, has tended to see its own security as dependent on political changes in the world as it is (although it, too, soon acquired a status quo to defend, especially in eastern Europe). It may be, of course, that in more recent years these roles have been changing; perhaps each side is coming to recognize a common interest in a certain kind of conservatism. Such trends would be important; for, as Michael Howard has said, "the maintenance of peace always depends on general agreement about the acceptability of the existing status quo."[54] And if such agreement could be obtained, even if it were qualified and partial, each side would see its security as closely tied to the security of the other side, the unilateral pursuit of national security would become less pronounced, and the great power relations of the future would thus have a different political dynamic from those of the past. Whether or not the future can be nudged in this direction remains, of course, to be seen.

Varieties of Threat

In the course of the arms competition that has been going on since 1945, each superpower has been inclined – and this is hardly unusual – to value very highly its own security requirements and to depreciate the fears of its rival. Neither has been much inclined to try to see the world from the other's point of view. Both have gone through times of heightened anxiety concerning national security. And fear has energized urgent action: the American military buildup in partial response to Sputnik; the Soviet attempt in 1962, partly in response to this buildup, to place missiles in Cuba; the recent accelerated American armaments program, which has been fuelled by fears for the future (such as the "window of vulnerability") and a desire to return to the more comforting Pax Americana of earlier years. Fearing an American attempt to regain nuclear superiority, the Kremlin has now, undoubtedly, authorized the development of new major weapons of its own. Fear, then, tends to feed upon fear, as each power seeks to enhance its own security by means of threatening actions directed at the other. And whatever else it might generate, such fear invariably results in the acquisition of more and more weapons, the further consolidation of military bureaucracies, and the hardening of confrontational concepts of international relations.

In the nuclear age fear has come to have a distinctive political significance. Now, for one's rival to be fearful is not necessarily a good thing. This truth is often insufficiently appreciated. As McGeorge Bundy, the national security advisor to Presidents Kennedy and Johnson, has remarked, "It is vital to understand that nuclear weapons scare other people more than they comfort the possessor. That's been true right from the beginning"[55] – and it may be getting truer with time. Nuclear weapons, by their very nature, are weapons of terror. They are not defensive; they provide no "shield" against attack. They offer, on their own, no reliable basis for security. They can only (it is hoped) deter through the threat of retaliation. But what one superpower calls its deterrent tends to be seen by the other side as a threat. And feeling threatened, it replies with new threatening weapons of its own.

This notion of "threat" pervades our thinking about the nuclear age. It is also one of the principal driving forces behind the arms race. Indeed, there is little doubt that this intense competition has been vigorously pushed along by both superpowers' alarmist, even morbid, assumptions about each other's intentions. (I shall look more closely at our understanding of the "Soviet threat" in the following chapter.) Each great power tends to attribute to the other power very large and aggressive objectives, and each then arms in order to meet these imagined, perhaps even imaginary, objectives. Analysts on both sides come up with worst-case scenarios concerning their own nation's security (this is done in part by highlighting the adversary's advantages while ignoring or deprecating one's own advantages). These scenarios invariably point to the need for large military deployments. And the deployments that result confirm the worst-case assessments of the analysts on the other side, who are thereby able to argue more convincingly for their own military programs. In this way the hawks on both sides feed on and help sustain one another. This process of interacting worst-case assessments makes a big contribution to driving the arms race onwards and upwards. As one American expert has remarked, "Our worst-case assessments, with our incomplete information, interact with Soviet worst-case assessments, and the result is a constant push upward, which is far, far stronger than any sort of downward pressures that political leaders are at all likely to exercise."[56]

There are two main dimensions to this interaction of worst-case assessments. (I am speaking here primarily of the United States, where, unlike the Soviet Union, public opinion and debate play a major role in the formulation of national security policy.) The first is what has become known as "threat inflation." This is the process by which the military capabilities of the enemy are seriously and persistently exaggerated – sometimes deliberately, sometimes less consciously. There is a long history of such threat inflation in American military circles. Soviet military strength has been repeatedly overrated, Soviet weaknesses and vulnerabilities have been time and again undervalued and disregarded.[57] The same sorts of claims regularly recur: "the Soviets are known to be developing ... ," "the Soviets have been deploying large numbers of ... ," "the Soviets may soon have the capacity to ... ." On these occasions little is usually said about the always formidable American capabilities. When efforts have been made to compare the forces on the two sides, the comparisons have frequently been misleadingly constructed and bolstered by the highly selective use of statistics. Normally they are designed largely to support those conclusions about "our" weakness and "their" might (with various associated demands for new military procurements) which have already been reached on less empirical grounds. Moreover, these sorts of threat assessments are usually reinforced by certain more-or-less unscrutinized assumptions about Soviet intentions, in particular, by a certain "hard" image of the other side's objectives. As Lawrence Freedman has demonstrated, such perceptions strongly informed the Pentagon's thinking in the late 1960s and early 1970s:

> The Pentagon's adversary image emphasised a Soviet drive to military superiority. All Soviet activity was interpreted by reference to this basic motivation. Any evidence of force modernisation was taken as confirmation of the basic thesis; any suggestion that Soviet objectives might be more moderate was dismissed as wishful thinking; any Soviet concessions in the SALT process were distrusted as an attempt to lull the West into a false sense of security. To military planners it seemed imprudent to make any reassuring assumptions as to the good sense and rationality of the adversary. Instead of emphasising the possibilities for arms control they took it to be their responsibility to warn of the dangers inherent in the negotiating process, and in particular the danger of prematurely lowering the military guard.[58]

Second, among many strategic and military planners there is a constant preoccupation with and publicizing of "vulnerabilities." The key element here is the creation of a sense of anxiety – anxiety that, because of certain alleged Western military deficiencies, Moscow might cease to be deterred ("in certain circumstances the Soviets might think they could succeed in..."); anxiety about what the enemy "can do to us" because of our supposed weaknesses, weaknesses that (it is said) can be remedied only through increased military expenditure. Much of this thinking is purely theoretical. It involves the abstracting of nuclear strategy from its political context. It is usually inattentive to the actualities of human purposes, political goals, and particular national traditions. Moreover, this search for vulnerabilities tends to take on a life of its own; it develops a capacity for self-reproduction. This process has been nicely observed with reference to the problem of ICBM vulnerability by Bernard O'Keefe, a man who has long and practical experience in nuclear weapons policy and production. He takes note of the suggestion that these missiles be made mobile, and points out what is likely to happen if this were done: "I have been around nuclear strategists for many years and I know how they think. I am certain that if the MX missiles are deployed in a mobile configuration, someone will write a paper suggesting that the Soviets could break the scheduling code [for moving the missiles]. Someone else would write a paper suggesting that since we don't know whether the Soviets could break the code or not, we should, for maximum security, assume that they could. This would open a new window of vunerability, and off we would go to a new level of escalation."[59]

Some of the vulnerabilities from the past have been largely or entirely imaginary: the bomber gap, the missile gap, the window of vulnerability. Others have had more substance, although they have, as a rule, been greatly exaggerated.[60] One might mention, for example, the long-standing tendency to overstate the inferiority of Western non-nuclear armaments relative to those of the Soviet Union and its Warsaw Pact allies. (This inferiority is the central justification for NATO's heavy reliance on nuclear weapons.) Soviet troop strength has been repeatedly exaggerated – sometimes grossly exaggerated.[61] It is now known that, as recently as the early 1980s, NATO's estimates of the size of the Soviet-bloc armies available for combat in Europe were almost 50 per cent too high.[62] Contrary to what is commonly thought, NATO's conventional forces have been formidable, especially since the early 1960s. NATO's total military manpower is roughly the same size as that of the Warsaw Pact, and the Soviet predominance in numbers of tanks is offset by the West's superiority in anti-tank weaponry. The standard scenario of a Soviet conventional attack on western Europe is highly implausible. Not only does the Soviet Union have nothing to gain from such an attack – its hands are already full in eastern Europe; why should it seek additional disgruntled and rebellious client states? – it does not possess the resources to have any confidence that it could succeed in such an extra-ordinary adventure.[63]

This is only one example of the common refrain of alarm, persistently over-dramatized. Even-handed and judicious official assessments of Soviet-American power relations have been the exception, not the norm. And this lack of coolness of judgment has been deeply rooted in fear: fear of a virtually boundless Soviet threat, fearful nervousness about newly discovered and often purely hypothetical vulnerabilities (which, it is assumed, the Soviets are sure to exploit), and, perhaps most important of all, a fear that America will cease to be, in its own eyes and in the eyes of the world, unambiguously number one.

The exploitation of fear is, of course, no new thing. Indeed, fear, if it can be "properly" defined and managed, has great political utility. As a prominent historian of u.s. foreign policy has recalled, John Foster Dulles was very conscious of the importance of keeping vigorously alive the idea of the "communist menace" and "liked to argue that the moment of greatest danger for the West would come when the perceived threat from the East had begun to fade – then allies would become quarrelsome, collective security arrangements would begin to seem outdated, neutralism would gain respectability. 'Fear,' he concluded, 'makes easy the tasks of diplomats.' "[64] The fear that Dulles had in mind pointed very much in a particular direction – in the direction of Moscow, not of the rapidly expanding nuclear arsenals themselves. Of course, fear of some adversary has always been one of the principal supports of any military establishment's identity and continued vitality. And in this respect one can recognize a keen mutuality of interest between the two dominant such establishments in the world of the late twentieth century. As Richard Barnet has noted,

> The military establishments in the United States and the Soviet Union are no doubt each other's best allies. The Soviets accommodate Pentagon budget planners by surfacing submarines, parading a new weapons system in Red Square, or writing bellicose articles in military journals ... Soviet military planners in turn, a Soviet general once told me, feed on the bellicose statements and extravagant budget projections that emanate from time to time from the Pentagon. Military bureaucracies, like any other, have a professional interest in keeping what they have, in enjoying the power and prestige of being at the frontiers of technology, and in projecting a threat that justi-

fies bigger budgets. (No market operates here. Threat is the substitute for consumer demand.)[65]

What we see nowadays, thinks another writer, is a kind of "tacit alliance between adversaries ... The military-industrial establishments on both sides cite the research and procurement of the other in justification of their demands for larger budgets and new programs." It may be that "in a number of branches Soviet and U.S. counterparts are in effect 'functional bureaucratic allies' and 'external pacers' for each other." They certainly help to justify each other's massive size. And the members of each national security establishment, especially the more hard-nosed, confrontational, and unaccommodating members, are greatly dependent on "the assistance of the adversary to provide support for their prophecies of doom and gloom."[66]

The distinguished historian William McNeill has remarked on how in the twentieth century these national security establishments have made use of fear to greatly expand their authority. For the past several decades, he writes, "military-industrial elites have nearly always prevailed over domestic rivals without much difficulty. Time and again fear of the foreign foe persuaded the political managers and the population at large to acquiesce in new efforts to match and overtake the other side's armament. The escalating arms race, in turn, helped to maintain conformity and obedience at home, since an evident outside threat was, as always, the most powerful social cement known to humankind."[67] This process continues. However, there is a new factor at work, a new fear, and that is the fear for the future of human life itself. And it is this fear – that weaponry has put survival fundamentally at risk – that is challenging and perhaps undermining the agenda of fear proposed by these military-industrial elites. Their threats are now not necessarily everyone's leading threats, and their definition of enemies may no longer be so readily and uncritically accepted. These differences in identifying and assessing threats have become central to the debates of the 1980s and are likely to continue so for many years to come.

Technological Momentum

While the political competition between the Soviet Union and the United States is obviously of central importance to the nuclear arms race, this race is now, perhaps, sustained as much by technological innovation as by political tensions. Indeed, the momentum of technological development has a definite life of it own, almost independent of the state of international or domestic politics at any given time. These technological changes occur quietly, out of the public view; they are often largely unknown to and unscrutinized by the elected policy-makers. As Deborah Shapley, an authority on this process, has suggested, "the capabilities of weapons seem to be shaped by the enthusiasm of scientists for advertising the potential of their work, the interest of program managers and design bureaus in testing improvements, and the armed services' wish to have the most up-to-date versions of their systems." This more or less self-generating technological momentum is produced largely by project engineers, systems managers, and bureaucrats, all of whom are continually trying to find ways to improve their weapons and to convince their superiors of the value of the work they are doing. Shapley calls this process "technology creep" in order to "emphasize its gradual, inconspicuous, bureaucratic character."[68]

The political impact of this technological momentum can be truly formidable, partly because it contributes to mutual fear and distrust, partly because of the immense domestic political power that has come to be exercised by the military-scientific-industrial establishments of both superpowers. Most of the results of military research are not particularly revolutionary; however, there is always the fear that the other side will produce some breakthrough, and even small innovations on one side create pressure for the other side to develop similar or superior capabilities. Once this technological dynamic becomes established, it develops its own impressive momentum, with political implications of considerable importance. The process has been well identified by the authors of *Common Security*: "Fear of technological inferiority causes nations to expand their military scientific establishments, thereby strengthening bureaucratic and corporate interests which favour a continuance of the arms race ... The technological competition contributes to doubts and suspicions on each side and, eventually, to the deterioration of political relations; this in turn leads to greater pressures for the development of new weapons. In other words, the race for technological sophistication and qualitative advantage becomes self-perpetuating."[69] This unceasing technological competition has been recognized by numerous observers and applauded by some. As General Curtis LeMay candidly put it, "Once the counter to a new weapon system has been invented and put into use, then, of course, the cycle repeats itself. And new offensive or defensive systems must be developed." This permanent arms race met with his approval.[70]

It is important to realize that much of this purely technological arms racing is *not* fundamentally reciprocal in character, especially in the United States, which generally has a lead in military technology. Rather than reacting to evidence of improving Soviet capabilities, the United States tends to move ahead technologically in order to ensure that, whatever the Soviets might actually do (of the various things it is imagined they could do), the United States will not be caught unprepared. And in devising new weapons American developers are, in fact, very often devising responses to their own emerging weapons, their own new military technologies, their own projected capabilities – capabilities that are routinely attributed to the adversary. "American planners," according to one authority, "tend to assume that the Soviets are engaged in any development program that the United States technical community has underway or has conceived of and are pursuing any technical avenue that has been identified as potentially fruitful or significant in the United States." Of course, the activities in Soviet laboratories are rarely known; and the "lack of hard data about Soviet development programs and the assumption that they are or could be doing whatever the United States is doing sometimes create the impression that the United States is competing with itself in strategic weaponry."[71] Partly because of the long lead time in the development of these weapon systems, perhaps eight to ten years from the drawing board to deployment, planners act on the basis of what they imagine might exist in the future; they invent and develop in anticipation of developments that (if they came to exist) would "require" a response. "What we do overall, in our military research and development," writes one American observer, "is to follow a policy of being number one, maintaining superiority, keeping ahead, doing the best one can. Such a process is, in an important sense, not at all interactive," that is, not at all dependent on what the Soviet Union is actually doing.[72] The challenges involved are mainly technical challenges. They sustain the careers and professional identities of tens of thousands of people. And as technicians respond to these challenges, as they are identified and anticipated, they are often actually trying to neutralize their own brain-children, the products of their own research centres and design bureaus.

This technological armaments race has produced a large constituency inherently in favour of its continuation. Hugh E. DeWitt, a physicist at the Lawrence Livermore National Laboratory in California, where many U.S. nuclear weapons are designed, has concluded that the scientists in the weapons laboratories "are a major force in driving and perpetuating the nuclear arms race." Many of these scientists, he reports, strongly believe "that high technology can provide safety and national security in a dangerous world" and that "technological solutions are paramount over political solutions."[73] Such special interests exert no mean influence in Washington. As Ted Greenwood has written of the American defence establishment (and much the same could be said of its Soviet counterpart): "Large organizations have been created that owe their continued existence solely to their ability to invent or design new weapons and sell them to political decision-makers. These organizations include not only the development commands of the services but also some of the largest of the nation's corporations who together employ millions of workers and represent a powerful political force."[74] These organizations (for instance, the giant aerospace corporations, hundreds of R & D centres) are deeply committed to maintaining their vitality, to seeking new challenges, to remaining vigorous and viable. In order to do so they have to devise promising new technical opportunities and get support for new projects. These institutional pressures that help to drive the arms race are strong and tenacious. "We are dealing here," asserts Wolfgang Panofsky, "with the institutional inertia or other manifestations of historical persistence that are inherent in any highly organized human activity. Institutions always find it difficult to produce only a fixed and limited amount of any one commodity; the producer always finds reasons why more of what he can produce is needed."[75] These institutional appetites for more and ever more are determined largely by domestic and bureaucratic politics, not by the current state of relations between nations. And the practical, mundane consequence of these pressures is that, as Richard Barnet has remarked, "Every weapons system comes off the drawing board with a built-in political coalition behind it."[76]

This alliance between science and the military has resulted in an arms race that, in the eyes of some critical commentators, has a kind of mad momentum of its own. They see it as a frenetic racing without end, a process with no real political purpose. Herbert York, an experienced observer of (and past participant in) the nuclear arms competition, has concluded that "It is not simply that the basic theory underlying the arms race is wrong, rather it is that there is no underlying theory at all."[77] Strategy itself has in many respects become the servant of the weapons makers. Politics is often taking a back seat to technological imperatives. This peculiar relationship between weaponry and politics in the nuclear age was remarked on some years ago by Hans Morgenthau. "There is in these technological developments," he thought, "a kind of inner logic – which is technologically rational but politically and militarily irrational – a technological dynamism which leads to ever more novelties, ever more improvements regardless of the military need and of the political consequences. In other words, what seems to be technologically possible is put into practice for no better reason but because it can be done."[78] Often new weapons are invented, and only then are missions found for them. New weaponry, it would seem, is not only determining much of the political agenda, it is actually, in many cases, outrunning politics. In short, we inhabit a world in which the military-technological tail is commonly wagging the political dog. Or, to change the metaphor, the servant threatens to dislodge the master.

Nuclear Symbolism

One final point. Nuclear weapons, in the contemporary world, are not simply physical realities. While they obviously embody vast destructive forces, they have also acquired a special significance in the world of human communications. For they have now become important symbols: symbols of power, status, and national prestige. They convey vital messages to others, messages that bespeak a special sort of domination and subordination. Whatever doubts may be felt about their practical utility, nuclear weaponry is, in essential respects, the principal currency of power in the modern world. It is the most awesome, the most exotic, the most exclusive of the various embodiments of power. As political currency, as a medium of symbolic exchange between states and as an overt expression of capability, it has been highly valued by its possessors, whatever problems they may have encountered in actually using it. It is a currency that the United States and the Soviet Union have struggled to manage and profit from. It underlines their special superpower status, their separation from all other states. They have, indeed, a common interest in keeping this currency as exclusive as possible and ensuring that, whatever bits of it might get into the hands of lesser nations, their own overwhelming superiority is maintained. The nuclear dimension is central to their great power status. However debased this nuclear currency might seem to be to its critics, however little "protection" it might seem to offer, and however unusable its physical power might seem to be, it is a currency that can play and has played a major role in the psychological dynamics of posturing between nations. It can be used to show who is boss, to remind lesser states of where power really lies, to display resolve, to distinguish clearly the key players from the rest. In the theatre of world politics, where imagery looms large and is assiduously cultivated, nuclear weapons derive significance, not only from the world of hardware, but also from the world of language – the world of symbolic exchange.

3
Civilization and Survival

But Surely Deterrence Has Worked?

It is often said that nuclear weapons have "kept the peace." Those, in particular, who wish to soothe the public's fears concerning the present nuclear arsenals point out that there has been no war between the great powers since 1945, and they attribute this absence of world war to the presence of these weapons of mass destruction. (Some assert that deterrence has kept the peace, but this is to misrepresent reality and reify an idea. Deterrence does not have a life of its own. It is the presence or absence of military force that, in this context, affects political action.) Had nuclear weapons not existed, according to some of these claims, a world war would probably have broken out by now. These weapons, it is said, have imposed a salutary restraint of terror on great power relations. More specifically, it is commonly asserted that, had the United States not enjoyed a monopoly of atomic weapons in the immediate post-war world, the Soviet Union would surely have used its military muscle to impose its will on all of Europe – indeed, perhaps even to overrun it. According to this view, it was only (or largely) because of the u.s. nuclear hegemony that Soviet power was contained and its aggressive expansionism held in check. On a broader level, one encounters the suggestion that nuclear weapons are a kind of blessing because of the paralysis they impose on the conduct of war; that their existence has made a major war so incredibly hazardous that no state will contemplate embarking on a path that would require the use of these weapons. Peace, then, is seen as the more or less assured product of universal fear. This view has been advanced by numerous commentators, among them the prominent American science writer William L. Laurence, who wrote in the late 1950s that "these very earth-destroying weapons make it practically certain that no nation, no matter how powerful, could dare risk an aggressive war, as such a war would mean only suicide for the aggressor ... The hydrogen bomb thus has made peace inevitable. It has achieved the realization of one of mankind's most cherished dreams – the abolition of large-scale, total wars of aggression."[1] Similarly, General Leslie Groves, the director of the wartime Manhattan Project, thought that once each great power came to possess "a full atomic arsenal" – as he believed had happened in the early 1960s – "major war is impossible. All that stands in the way of effective international control is the acceptance by all the world's political leaders of this fact."[2]

It would be hard to deny, I think, that nuclear weapons have induced statesmen to act with special caution. The increasing industrialization of warfare had already, before 1945, made warfare a total experience and allowed the attainment of unprecedented levels of destruction. With the advent of nuclear weapons, this trend took a quantum leap upwards. After 1945, when thoughtful people reflected on the devastation that had been suffered in the Second World War, they could contemplate as well the much greater destructive power that might be unleashed and probably would be unleashed in any future great-power struggle. These realities were bound to prompt rulers to tread warily. Peace came to be very highly valued, in both rhetoric and substance, if only because the price of warfare had clearly become so catastrophic. Preventing a conflict between the superpowers came to be regarded by many people as the paramount goal in world affairs. Preserving, at the least, a kind of stand-off between the Soviet Union and the United States seemed critically important. Both superpowers have tended to act very cautiously in arenas where there was any sort of risk of directly confronting the other, and each has acted much more boldly when such a confrontation appeared unlikely. As one historian has said of the Soviet Union in the period since 1945, "however Soviet leaders have viewed their relations with the United States and whatever their ultimate aspirations for communism, in the realm of practical politics they have been far more willing to risk the use of military force to maintain territories and spheres of influence than to attain new ones, too fearful of the consequences of general war to run the risk of its outbreak."[3] The Cuban missile affair in 1962 is the exception that highlights the general rule. Similarly, the United States, which has been quick to intervene militarily in many Third World nations, has shown little disposition to challenge the Soviet Union's territorial gains after the Second World War or its continuing domination of the countries of eastern Europe.

None of these reflections, however, necessarily leads to the conclusion that "nuclear weapons have kept the peace," which is a much larger and rather dogmatic contention. Indeed, this oft-repeated claim is remarkably evasive about a number of questions. Is it possible that the absence of war might be explained in other, equally plausible ways? Is there any evidence that warlike intentions were actually deterred by nuclear force? And can the experiences of the past four decades really be taken as testimony to the "deterrent" power of nuclear weapons?

Let us begin by recalling the circumstances of political life at the end of the Second World War, when Soviet military forces, as a result of their victories over German fascism, were able to occupy much of eastern and central Europe and ensure that suitably reliable governments were established in these states. (There were exceptions, as in Austria and Yugoslavia.) After Soviet troops had captured Nazi-held territory, they demonstrated a determination to exploit the power vacuum that usually existed and to stay long enough to create a new state apparatus that would be compatible with Leninist principles. But did the Soviet Union intend to take over western Europe? Is there any evidence that Soviet leaders were contemplating an early war with the West? While keeping in mind the uncertainties that are bound to surround such questions, partly because of the opaqueness of Kremlin decision-making, what we can say, I think, is that *there is no evidence* of Soviet intentions of war against the West; that, as Herbert Butterfield once remarked, "there seems to be no reason for believing that Russia would have meditated a full-scale war, even if she had had to meet only pre-atomic weapons, the weapons of Hitler's war";[4] and that there has always been a great deal of well-informed scepticism about the prospect of further Soviet expansion so soon after the collapse of the Nazi regime – a scepticism that deserves to be more actively kept in mind and recollected than is often now the case.

This scepticism as to the peace-keeping functions attributed to nuclear weapons has been informed by a variety of considerations and advanced by a diverse assortment of political commentators. One of the most thoughtful of these alternative arguments to explain the absence of war after 1945 has been offered by the late Raymond Aron, a political observer with no love for Communism and a long record of opposition to Soviet state power. Aron thought that, with regard to the five or six years after the defeat of Hitler, "It would be most difficult to attribute any major influence on international relations to these [nuclear] weapons. To be sure," he continued,

> there were, and still may be, observers firmly convinced that the Red Army would have occupied all of Western Europe in 1945 or 1946 had it not been for the atom bomb. This hypothesis, though it cannot be conclusively disproved (how can one prove that what did not happen would have happened if one circumstance had been different?), strikes me as extremely unlikely. Soviet cities lay in ruins, the country's economy had to be rebuilt, and Eastern Europe had to be absorbed into the Soviet system. And even if Britain and the United States had actually demobilized their armies – which they might not have done without an atomic monopoly – I still wonder whether Stalin would have risked a third World War on the perilous assumption that, having gone to war to keep Hitler from unifying Europe under Nazi rule, the British and Americans would idly stand by and watch him carry out the *Führer's* grand design.[5]

As Aron had remarked in an earlier book, "if we ask whether the fate of Europe would have been different without the atom bomb, two obvious questions arise: Even if it had not had the bomb, would the United States have tolerated the expansion of the Soviet empire as far as the Atlantic? And would Stalin have been ready to face the risk of general war?"[6] What also needs to be recalled is that most Western experts, in the immediate post-war years, did *not* expect a Soviet attack on western Europe, did *not* see the "Communist threat" as primarily a military threat, and did *not* think that Moscow wanted war.[7] Even the CIA, in a study of 1950, questioned the assertion that "only the existence of the U.S. atomic bomb prevented the USSR from carrying out an intention to continue its military advance to the Atlantic"; the report thought that "there is no reason to suppose ... that the USSR had any such intention in 1945 or subsequently."[8]

There are, then, numerous reasons for doubting that war was likely in the second half of the 1940s, even had nuclear weapons not existed. There clearly existed, as E.P. Thompson has said, "a very considerable disinclination to embark on any course that would make possible World War Three, whether nuclear or not."[9] The Soviet Union was, of course, in a greatly weakened state. Given what it had endured between 1941 and 1945, it had every reason to avoid war and to look forward to a time of peace; time that would allow it to rebuild its shattered economy and strive to diminish the huge technological-industrial gap that existed between itself and the United States. It was simply not in a fit state to try to extend its power by further conquest. (It could not expect to find the sort of stark power vacuums further west that had made its take-overs in eastern Europe relatively easy.) Moreover, certain Soviet actions were incompatible with any intent to make war on the West. "All through 1946," as Richard Barnet has recalled, "the Soviet Union continued to tear up the railroad track across East Germany. Feverish dismantling of this sort was consistent with Stalin's preoccupation of the moment – the rise of a revanchist Germany within a generation – but not with any secret plan to march west." He comments as well that, "With all the disclosures of Stalin's crimes by post-Stalinist politicians and Soviet defectors, it is noteworthy that not one bit of evidence has emerged indicating that Stalin planned a military attack on Western Europe in the late nineteen-forties."[10] Had Stalin actually been seriously thinking about moving further west, it is difficult to believe that Soviet forces would have been demobilized to the extent that they were – a demobilization that reduced the number of Soviet men in arms by almost 75 per cent during the two years after 1945.

Implicit in the contention that nuclear weapons have kept the peace is the suggestion that, had there been no such bombs, the West would have been unable to resist Soviet aggression (let us, for argument's sake, assume such aggression). Although this reasoning is rarely spelled out, the implication is that there was probably no alternative credible defence policy available to the Western democracies, that is, that there were no satisfactory non-nuclear strategies for defence against Soviet attack. But this claim is so preposterous that it is hard to take it seriously. After all, in 1945 the conventional military strength of the Western Allies was substantially greater than that of Russia: they had more men in the armed forces, much more imposing air power, and incomparably superior industrial capacity. Stalin could hardly have been unaware of such strengths. And those strengths that were specifically military in character could, of course, have been sustained at considerably higher levels than they actually were, had it been thought necessary to do so. "If no atomic bombs had existed," observed the physicist and writer on military affairs P.M.S. Blackett a few years later, "and if a Soviet land attack in Europe had been feared, then the Western Allies would undoubtedly have slowed down their demobilization and kept larger conventional forces in Europe. In the first years after the War, the few atomic bombs in existence were not needed to save Western civilization from Communist aggression."[11] The fact that an alternative defence posture, which could have been non-nuclear in character, was not seriously developed was largely a consequence of the existence of the American atomic arsenal and the mighty confidence that was placed in this "advantage."

One of the ironies in all this talk about the atomic restraint that was imposed on Soviet leaders is that the USSR made most of its territorial gains during those years when it had no nuclear arsenal at all. It consolidated its hold over eastern Europe entirely during the period of the American nuclear monopoly. Very few of its gains have been achieved since 1949. Moreover, as Raymond Aron once observed, "throughout the era of unilateral deterrence" (the five or six years after 1945) "it was, as a rule, the Soviet Union that called the signals... All through this period it was as though the Soviet Union decided to make up for its manifest inferiority in atomic arms by an equally manifest aggressive hostility." He suggests that one might have to seek an explanation for such action in terms of "the paradox posed by the aggressiveness of the weaker."[12] There seems, certainly, to be no positive correlation between Soviet political success and its strength in nuclear weaponry. McGeorge Bundy thinks that "the real correlation is always the one between applicable Soviet influences of all sorts and the situation on the spot. Some of these situations have allowed Soviet influence to grow," he notes, but others have not. And it was, he points out, during the later 1960s and early 1970s, when "their [nuclear] arsenal was growing most rapidly that the Soviets suffered their greatest reverses – in China, in Indonesia, and in Egypt. And on our side," he adds, addressing his American audience, "it is worth remembering that the one instrument of influence that is entirely irrelevant in Central America is the bomb."[13] These various considerations are rarely addressed by those who stress the alleged political utility of nuclear weapons and the beneficial role they have played.

There are, it is clear, a number of possible reasons that a major war has been avoided, only one of which – and not necessarily the most plausible – emphasizes the impact of nuclear weapons. It should be recognized that all these proposed explanations are strictly hypothetical. None of them can be proved. Those who hold to the view that "deterrence has worked" should be advised to recall that, as Abba Eban has observed, "Deterrence is the strategy of *dissuading* an adversary from taking undesirable action, and since it is a passive concept it is impossible to prove."[14] The non-occurrence of something could have been for all sorts of reasons, and testing such causal hypotheses empirically is always a very tenuous enterprise. Those who assert that nuclear weapons have kept the peace are, in essence, merely expressing an article of faith. They may believe but they cannot demonstrate. The epistemological reality we confront has been pointed out in colloquial language by the authors of a book on the American defence establishment: "there is no way to tell if deterrence is working. It's like the old joke about the clown who keeps snapping his fingers to keep the wild elephants away. Must work, he figures. No wild elephants here. We'll never know for certain. But we will know all too well if deterrence fails."[15]

While there can be no doubt that the fear surrounding nuclear weapons has inhibited their actual use, this fear has done little if anything to discourage their mass production. Whatever deterrence may or may not have done, it has certainly not prevented the extraordinary *preparations* for war that we have witnessed since 1945. There are now some 45,000 to 50,000 nuclear warheads in the world, approximately 27,000 of which are in American possession (the USSR has most of the rest). These military buildups have proceeded in a seemingly inexorable manner, continually achieving new and greater heights of technological sophistication. And in recent years these buildups have been persistently justified in terms of the supposed need to "strengthen our deterrent." However it may be related to the keeping of peace, deterrence thinking has certainly contributed vigorously to the ongoing, largely unchecked process of the nuclear arms competition and the drive to accumulate, first, more and more weapons, and more recently, increasingly sophisticated weapons. This nuclear arms race, however it might be explained or defended, has resulted in a precarious state of affairs; for, as Jonathan Schell has remarked, "behind the screen of our deterrence policy we have built the means of our annihilation." Peace, it seems, has been firmly tied to what threatens to undo us. However one might feel about this situation, complacency is certainly not in order. Schell has employed a metaphor to represent our present condition of existence. "If someone climbs out on a ledge of a high building and threatens to jump off, we do not stand around congratulating him on his wisdom and restraint in not having jumped yet, and expounding on how safe a place the ledge of a building must be; we seek to pull him in at the earliest possible opportunity."[16] Clearly, being perched on the precipice is not an ideal vantage-point for the conduct of national security policy.

Scepticism, then, is warranted when dealing with some of the explanations currently offered as to the absence thus far of nuclear war. This scepticism was already being expressed early in the nuclear age, before deterrence theory had been much developed. In 1948 P.M.S. Blackett predicted what was likely to happen if American atomic bombs came to be regarded as the main deterrent to Soviet expansion. "For suppose that no Russian aggression, say by expansion over the Yalta line, does take place in the next few years, and suppose further that this lack of aggression is widely held in the West as due to the threat of atomic bombing, then the West will, in its own view, have saved the world from a third world war, at any rate for some years."[17] One cannot help but think that this argument that Blackett foresaw, which has indeed come to be widely espoused, is especially congenial partly because it serves to justify past policies, notably policies that were responsible for a highly nuclearized concept of national security. This concept of "strength" highlighted, as it still does, the nuclear component, while playing down other sources of a nation's strength and other possible paths to security – paths that were avoided and not pursued. So much emphasis has been placed on the role of nuclear weaponry in Western defence policy that many people have a strong vested interest in believing that it *has* worked, that the pronounced nuclearization of strategy has been a great success. This is not to imply that the policies that were followed necessarily achieved what their authors wanted to achieve. Most American military planners in the late 1940s and early 1950s did not anticipate or look forward to a world of *mutual* assured destruction, with its inhibiting implications for U.S. armed forces (Bernard Brodie was an exception), but that is what quickly materialized. Some of the arguments we now hear about the success of deterrence are simply ways of making a virtue of the partly unforeseen consequences of past actions, notably the rapid development of a huge Soviet nuclear arsenal, mirroring that of the United States.

One further point on this issue. There is at least a hint in some of these official representations of the past that as long as we maintain deterrence in the future all will be well, or at least as well as can be expected. Past success, it is suggested, should be allowed to guide our future actions. If deterrence has kept the peace, then surely it can continue to keep the peace. This contention, of course, assumes that deterrence can be more or less permanently preserved, that it can be made effective and workable over the very long term. Such an assumption would not be easy to defend. Few policies can be expected to work perfectly, and yet deterrence depends on perfection: on error-free conduct, indefinitely observed. Few things, we know, are permanent in relations between sovereign states. To expect a permanent stand-off in a highly militarized relationship between two great powers is to ask for a lot. We know, moreover, from consulting historical experience, that large stockpiles of weapons almost always get used, sooner or later. To hope that present arsenals will remain permanently unused may be wishful thinking. While we might be grateful, then, that we have managed to survive four decades of the nuclear age, it may be that future survival will require different policies from those that have got us where we now are, different concepts of security, and different approaches to the conduct of world politics.

The Soviet Threat

In Western countries we hear a great deal about "the Soviet threat." This threat is, in certain respects, undoubtedly real. Any great power is, always has been, and will continue to be feared by others. The repressive and often brutal domination of the countries of eastern Europe by the USSR and its insistence, intermittently backed by guns, that these countries mechanically toe the Communist party line are so manifest for all to see that they can be regarded as beyond dispute. Soviet leaders, at the end of the Second World War, grabbed all that they could of Hitler's former empire, and, with the aim of better securing Russia's western borders against any future invasion, they resolved to retain political control of most of these lands and since then have shown little sign of being disposed to relax their grip. (Such generalizations do conceal important differences. Bulgaria, a very poor country in 1945, has, on balance, perhaps benefited from state-directed economic development; and present-day Hungary shows signs of being a vigorous society. Poland and Czechoslovakia, in contrast, have had much less happy histories.) Official Soviet ideology is, of course, hostile to Western capitalist freedoms; indeed, it posits, at least in some of its stricter Leninist versions, a relationship with the rest of the world that is harshly adversarial. The Soviet state itself is decidedly secretive, authoritarian, and intolerant of dissent; and its own model for economic development, which emphasizes centralized planning and structures of command, has been winning considerably fewer admirers in recent years. Many people in the West have come to think that the Soviet system is a new form of barbarism and that the only language its leaders understand is the language of intimidation and violence. In these circles the Soviet Union is seen as inherently aggressive, intent on further conquest, and largely indifferent to human suffering. These dangerous ambitions are commonly contrasted with Western – especially American – virtue, righteousness, and benign intent. Former U.S. President Richard Nixon was undoubtedly speaking for many Americans when he said, in 1983, that "the struggle between the Soviet Union and the United States is between an avowedly and manifestly aggressive power and an avowedly and manifestly defensive one. The United States," he asserted, "wants peace; the Soviet Union wants the world."[18]

The Soviet buildup of nuclear arms since the mid-1960s is undeniable. What is at issue is the complex of objectives that underlies Soviet military policy. One prominent view asserts that the USSR is striving for nuclear superiority in order to be able to emerge victorious from some future nuclear conflict with the West. This position, which has been commonplace on the American political right, was vigorously advanced by, among others, Richard Pipes, a Harvard academic and frequent adviser to U.S. policy-makers, in an influential article first published in 1977 entitled "Why the Soviet Union Thinks It Could Fight and Win a Nuclear War." According to Pipes, "The strategic doctrine adopted by the USSR over the past two decades calls for a policy diametrically opposite to that adopted in the United States by the predominant community of civilian strategists: not deterrence but victory, not sufficiency in weapons but superiority, not retaliation but offensive action."[19] Claims that run in this direction, though not always quite so wholeheartedly, came to be widely accepted in Washington. Defense Secretary Caspar Weinberger, for example, in an opinion recorded in mid-1983, represented Soviet thinking in the following way:

> Unfortunately, we are faced with an adversary who does not necessarily share our abhorrence of war, even nuclear war. In fact, there is ample evidence that the Soviets have a very different view, and that they regard nuclear weapons as no different than other weapons. The Soviet leadership, through its actions, force deployments, and writings, has in fact given us the clear perception that it believes a nuclear war may be fought and won under certain circumstances.[20]

If Soviet leaders truly think this way – if they actually reject deterrence, acknowledge no clear distinction between conventional and nuclear weapons, and (it is also assumed) are deeply committed to the expansion of their empire – then surely, as Weinberger, Pipes, and many others believe, the United States has no choice but to respond in kind, to demonstrate the utmost resolve, and to prepare adequately for whatever aggression the Soviet Union might have in mind.

But do Soviet leaders hold such views? Does Soviet military thinking really conceive of nuclear war in such a casual manner? Numerous Western experts on the USSR have been scrutinizing the propositions of Pipes and like-minded observers in the light of the fairly abundant evidence concerning Soviet military doctrine. And what these studies show, quite compellingly in my view, is that Soviet doctrine *does* accept the fact of mutual deterrence, that it regards nuclear war as almost certainly catastrophic, and that it strongly favours restraints on the arms race, although it is also true that the deterministic premises of official Soviet ideology ("socialism will triumph") discourage a completely open admission that, in the nuclear age, socialism is just as likely to be obliterated as capitalism. To cite just one of the many authorities on this question, John Erickson of the University of Edinburgh, a leading Western expert on Soviet military affairs, has recently concluded, "On the whole, Soviet opinion seems to hold that nuclear war is *not* a rational instrument of policy, for means and ends lose any significance when the cost of destroying the enemy amounts to self-annihilation ... Soviet deterrent policies are designed to minimize the incentives for attacking the USSR and, above all, are aimed at preventing the outbreak of hostilities."[21] The emphasis in recent Soviet writing has been very much on the horrors of nuclear war, the unparalleled disasters that it would bring, and the set-backs that socialism would suffer as a result of any such conflict. The special character of nuclear weapons has been increasingly recognized; and Lenin's assertions as to the inevitability of war have been largely, if not entirely, abandoned. There is much evidence that Soviet leaders clearly recognize the vulnerability of their society to nuclear destruction and wish to minimize the risk of such a catastrophe. They see competition with capitalism as inevitable, but they are clearly nervous about the nuclear arms race and would much prefer to pursue competition in other ways. Evidence that they are complacent about nuclear war and its potential implications is decidedly thin.[22] Indeed, one well-informed observer of Soviet affairs, and a frequent visitor to that country, Seweryn Bialer, thinks that "fear of such a [nuclear] holocaust among Soviet leaders, elites, and peoples is much more real, much more tangible, than in the United States."[23]

In trying to make sense of the debate in the West as to what the Kremlin and its military advisers think about the utility of nuclear weapons, several cautionary remarks are in order. First, in Soviet writings there is much ritual genuflecting in the direction of the laws of Marxism-Leninism, and since these laws did not foresee the possibility of a nuclear holocaust, it is not always easy for Communist writers to reconcile or even to confront explicitly the claims of political dogma (such as the historical inevitability of socialist advance) and the facts of modern technology. Consequently, Soviet writing often has to be read on two levels: on the level of keeping the ideological faith, which is central to all approved Soviet views of the world; and on the level of empirically informed observation of the world as it now exists, which frequently breaks through the rigidity of doctrinal pronouncements and informs much actual Soviet international conduct (such as the willingness to negotiate arms control agreements).

Second, while Soviet military writings tend to focus explicitly on war-fighting problems, including those that might be involved in nuclear war, this emphasis is no different from that in American military thought, which has always emphasized how to fight and win wars, including nuclear wars. If there is any significant distinction to be made, it is not that between Soviet and American military doctrine, but rather the distinction between the traditions of military thought on both sides, which have always focused on the conduct of war (on the assumption that peace has ended), and the priorities of politicians on both sides, whose common fundamental concern has become the prevention of war. The importance of recognizing the distinction between military and political concerns in Soviet thinking has been properly stressed by Seweryn Bialer: "If Soviet *military* doctrinal writings treat nuclear war in terms of a winning strategy, the authoritative Soviet *political* writings never raise this theme. Quite the opposite, [for] it is clear from these political writings that such a war is viewed as an utter disaster, a total failure of basic Soviet policies, an outcome that has to be avoided at all costs. The increasing military strength of the Soviet Union and its allies is seen as the best deterrent to such a war."[24] David Holloway has clarified this distinction in the following way:

> The political side of Soviet doctrine stresses the importance, and the possibility, of preventing a war between the socialist and capitalist camps. The military side attends to the question of waging and winning such a war, "if the imperialists should unleash it" (to use the standard Soviet qualification).* Consequently, deterrence is a political rather than a military concern, and receives almost no attention in Soviet military writings. Soviet doctrine sees the prevention of war as something to be achieved by means of a "peace policy" – that is, a foreign policy which seeks to reduce the risks of war – backed by Soviet military might.[25]

Third, it is ironic to realize that, if there have been failures to distinguish adequately between nuclear and non-nuclear weapons, and if there have been efforts to make nuclear weapons seem "conventional" and unremarkable, these undesirable modes of thinking originated and have been most actively cultivated, not in the Soviet Union, but rather in the United States (as we saw in the previous chapter), mostly during the years of overwhelming American nuclear

---

*American military planners employ similar thinking and a similar formula: elaborate plans have been made to conduct and prevail in a nuclear war, on the assumption that "Soviet aggression" forces the United States to fight.

supremacy. Whether or not Soviet experts have expressed any wry amusement about the charges now flung in their direction is not yet known to us.

Fourth and finally, it is noticeable that the assertions about Soviet nuclear-war-fighting commitments have stemmed largely from the American political right (scholars of Soviet affairs with no obvious axe to grind, such as those cited in the notes to this discussion, have presented quite different and much more subtle conclusions). This is noteworthy, for these are also the people who have been pushing U.S. nuclear strategy towards a more active and assertive war-fighting posture, and one of their justifications for this shift is the alleged existence of explicit Soviet war-winning nuclear doctrines, which, they say, have to be resisted with like American doctrines. In this way, it seems, are changing emphases in Western strategy defended by reference to simplistic and sometimes even largely imaginary representations of Soviet views.

The evidence available on Soviet doctrine, and the testimony of many informed Western commentators, is overwhelmingly incompatible with those arguments that presume a pursuit by the Soviet Union of nuclear superiority. There is a din of voices on the subject of the Soviet Union, and separating the sensible observers from the ideologues is not always easy. Some voices command respect and serious consideration; others do not. Among the more thoughtful and judicious interpreters of Soviet conduct is Raymond Garthoff, a long-standing expert on Soviet military affairs and a former U.S. ambassador to Bulgaria. In remarks made in 1982 Garthoff addressed himself to the suggestion that the USSR is seeking military superiority over the United States. "In my judgment," he said,

> the Soviets are not pursuing military superiority; by that I mean they do not believe that they will be able, under present or foreseeable circumstances, to achieve military superiority. They would like to have an edge over us, just as we would like to have an edge over them, and this judgment does not mean that they are not going to continue to pursue very active military programs that we have to consider very seriously. Nevertheless, they affirm that they are not seeking military superiority, and I think that's probably true, not because they say it, but, if you wish, despite the fact that they say it.

He went on to point to what he saw as the reality of Soviet attitudes in the present state of world politics:

> Although we talk about Soviet superiority, I believe the Soviet leaders see the current situation as a precarious state of parity that has been achieved in the last decade. They think the United States is seeking to regain superiority and are afraid that we may, in fact, gain or think we have gained such an edge by the end of this decade. So they see parity, if not as an optimum objective, then as the preferred objective to what they see as the most likely alternative, a return to some degree of American superiority, which they fear we would then use to reinforce a political policy of intimidation.[26]

Such Soviet fears and concerns need to be accorded much more attention than they generally are. They also help to explain why Soviet leaders have attached such importance to detente, as the most promising path to national security. Detente, for them, is a means of mitigating their sense of being beleaguered, of stabilizing their nation's status as the other great power, and of reducing the chance of direct confrontation with the United States (a nation that they regard very ambivalently, as both a rival and a model – at least in certain technological and economic respects – of what to strive for). It was during the years of detente that Soviet leaders came to feel most secure. They have, then, good reason for wanting to continue (or, now, to revive) these policies and to rest content with a kind of status quo, if only because, as Seweryn Bialer has remarked, "The Soviets surely know that without detente, in an uncontrolled arms race, they cannot hope to secure [strategic superiority] ... owing to the size, strength, and decisive technological superiority of the American and Western economies ... Moreover, an uncontrolled arms race would dramatically maximize all the dangers of escalating confrontations which the Soviet Union wishes to avoid as much as the United States."[27]

Soviet leaders, in short, have favoured detente because it was prudent and sensible to do so, in their national self-interest. In the mid-1970s, Robert Kaiser, who reported from Moscow for the *Washington Post*, expressed the view that "Soviet leaders opt for negotiations because they cannot profit from all-out competition ... Isolated, economically far inferior to the capitalist West, tied to a vulnerable empire and wary of a hostile China, the Russians would be

rash indeed to willingly engage the best energies of their adversaries."
He felt that detente "represents a fundamental decision about the best
way the Soviet Union can achieve its international objectives, the first
of which is security from hostile forces."[28] These remarks have lost no
force today. In the face of many representations to the contrary from
Western military spokesmen, it is wise to remember that most Soviet
leaders, whatever their distrust of the West, and whatever repression
they may promote within their own borders and in eastern Europe,
regard the existing state of mutual deterrence as preferable to an
unstable, ongoing, economically exhausting competition for nuclear
superiority. Their frequently declared satisfaction with parity is, then,
decidedly credible.

Russian Insecurities

Distorted perceptions of Soviet policy and outlook are regrettably
commonplace in the West, and these misapprehensions work very
much against efforts to formulate sensible policy and, in the end, they
have dangerous implications for our common survival. We hear much
of Soviet hostility but little about the official, long-standing Soviet
policy of coexistence with the West. (Soviet doctrine holds that
socialism will spread without war with the West.) We are often told
about Soviet "expansionism," and there is no doubt that Russia has
wanted and endeavoured to spread its influence, as have all great
powers, past and present, including the United States. (A desire to
spread influence does not necessarily imply a plot to rule the world.)
However, it is also clear that, since its take-over of much of eastern
Europe at the end of the Second World War, the Soviet Union has, in
terms of direct political control, expanded very little. Its "empire" is
not much larger now than it was in 1950, and if it has gained influence
in a few regions, it has lost influence elsewhere (Egypt, Indonesia,
China). Of course, when conflict erupts somewhere on the globe, we
are often encouraged to look for – even assume – some guiding Soviet
hand at work. But it should now be obvious that most of the bloody
struggles of recent times have been kinds of civil war, wars in which
the Soviet Union has usually played only a secondary or reactive role,
or none at all. (Afghanistan is the only major exception.)

Many Western observers, in fact, regard Soviet foreign policy as
remarkably conservative, unadventurous, and pragmatic – and on the

whole not particularly successful. It is, they agree, much more cautiously opportunistic than systematically expansionist. According to Stanley Hoffmann, a judicious interpreter of international affairs, "there is no Soviet master plan," no blueprint for the systematic spreading of Soviet power. Indeed, defensive motives play a much larger role in Soviet policy than many Westerners are prepared to allow. A fundamental proposition about Soviet conduct, as Hoffmann puts it, is that "the Soviet Union still has an overriding fear of encirclement, and is determined to preempt any attempt at enclosure."[29] This fear of encirclement is crucial to Soviet views of the outside world, and critically informs its pursuit of global "equality." "The Russians," observes Robert Kaiser, "have behaved like people who want to be taken more seriously on the world stage, who crave recognition as the second and co-equal super-power. Their eagerness for status and influence is troublesome, sometimes dangerous, but less worrisome than an actively aggressive, expansionist Soviet policy would be. Like the rest of us," he thinks, "they are principally interested in protecting themselves"[30] – a not surprising priority, considering the Russians' experiences of being invaded (as well as their invading others).

I do not wish to suggest that the Soviet threat is non-existent. The question is what one makes of it. The world is full of threats, only one of which stems from Soviet state power. Moreover, in the West, as I noted in chapter two, this power is continually inflated. Soviet military strengths are exaggerated, Soviet weaknesses are ignored or at least vastly under-publicized. Consider the following points. The total wealth of NATO members is at least three times that of the Warsaw Pact. NATO, a defensive alliance, has as many men in arms as the Warsaw Pact (any successful offensive against such a defensive alliance would require a large margin of force superiority, perhaps on the order of three to one). Military technology in the Soviet bloc is generally qualitatively inferior – sometimes greatly inferior – to that in the West. The United States is still superior to the Soviet Union in all major categories of nuclear weaponry except land-based missiles. The Soviet Union has few willing allies and its international political position is, if anything, deteriorating. And it has to assign some 20 per cent of its military establishment to securing its border with China, another, yet hostile, Communist state that has sometimes been suspected by Soviet leaders of moving towards an alliance with the United States.

We hear not nearly enough about such limitations on Soviet power – limitations that are critical to any overall assessment of "the Soviet threat." A major part of our difficulty in realistically assessing Soviet power was pointed out a few years ago by Robert Kaiser. The West, he said, "has persistently overestimated the threat posed by Soviet military strength, and so generally ignored the implications of the country's weaknesses in non-military fields … we have given the Russians more than their due credit for military prowess, and ignored their failings in economic and technological development, social organization and the rest. We have defined strength and power in purely military terms – the terms most favorable to the Soviet Union – and then exaggerated Soviet power."[31]

It is often said that the West can negotiate with the Russians only from a position of strength. In fact, the West has always enjoyed such strength. The fear that we are not strong is largely a result of inflated assessments of Soviet military power, of a determination in certain circles to discount Western advantages, and of melodramatic and fanciful imaginings of a surprise Soviet attack against NATO or some vital Western interest. There is in all this talk a pronounced tendency to dwell inordinately on what military move the Soviets could make if they were to act in a spirit of explosive midsummer madness, rather than on what they are likely to do in pursuit of their own self-interest. And there is, I think, in these morbid and rather silly scenarios of unprovoked Soviet attack, an implicit assumption that the Soviet leadership might well act some day with wild abandon and totally uncharacteristic recklessness, throwing all caution to the winds. Such unbalanced, alarmist, and often contorted thinking is not only an impediment to sensible policy. It also fosters the sort of public anxiety that leads to the increasing militarization of international politics, the continual fuelling of the arms race, and the undermining of all efforts for arms control.

Misreadings of Soviet policies and objectives and Soviet misreadings of Western politics and commitments have been so commonplace and recurrent that one wonders if statesmen will ever be able to break out of stereotypes that have so frequently stunted their diplomacy. Time and time again circumstances have arisen in which each side is essentially deaf to the views of the other: it is simply assumed that "they" are at fault and acting aggressively, and that "we" – whether "we" are in Moscow or Washington – are in the right and merely acting defensively. Consider, for example, the deployment of a new generation of land-based medium-range missiles in Europe. NATO viewed the Soviet deployment of ss-20s as threatening, provocative, and destabilizing, as an effort to gain political advantage in Europe. Soviet leaders, in contrast, saw their new missiles as an improved deterrent against the hostile nuclear forces that were close to Soviet borders and owned by four different nations. They regarded the new American deployments, the ground-launched cruise missiles and Pershing IIs, as an increase in the U.S. strategic arsenal, since all their warheads could hit Soviet territory, and thus a circumventing of at least the spirit of the SALT agreements. Each side, in this debate as in many that preceded it, displayed little capacity for understanding or even trying to understand why the other side was acting and thinking as it was.[32] Each, for the most part, assumed the worst of the other and justified its own actions in terms of defensive requirements. As Marshall Shulman pointed out in 1983, one of the problems complicating U.S.-Soviet relations is "the tendency to view the actions and statements of one's own side with indulgence and those of the other side with severity. That tendency is particularly strong during periods of tension and nationalism, like today." Self-righteousness, the easy presumption of moral superiority, however successful it might be in helping people feel better about themselves, almost always undermines good judgment and subverts the restrained conduct of international relations. This "is not to say," remarks Shulman, "that the differences between the superpowers are only a matter of perception – they are real, and they are serious – but that distortions in the way the two countries perceive each other exacerbate the differences and make more difficult the sensible management of the competition between them."[33]

These distortions of Russian views of the West, and of Western – especially American – views of the Soviet Union, undoubtedly have diverse cultural and political roots. But if one were to try to identify an especially fundamental difference between the Soviet Union and the United States, which is deeply rooted in their radically contrasting histories, one might point, I think, to the Russian sense of tragedy and of recurrent suffering and harsh endurance, as distinct from the American sense of optimism, self-confidence, and competitive success. Russians are acutely aware of their tumultuous and often cruel past, of the many sacrifices that have been made for the sake of their nation's security, of the fragility of their present position in a generally hostile world. They have suffered greatly in war, and tens of millions have been victimized, in some way or other, as they found themselves a prey to organized violence, either internal or external. Russian history, a story dominated by insecurity, crisis, and periodic disaster, is dramatically unlike the history of the United States. Russia, thinks one writer, "is a land with a poignant history of survival," and one of the results of this history, he suggests, is that "Russians are deeply attached to their miseries as well as to their joys. Their literature and music have made an artistic pleasure of sadness."[34] American culture, in contrast, is almost totally lacking a tragic sense (at least outside the southern states). It is a culture that stresses buoyancy, cheerfulness, and a sense of limitless opportunity. Americans have tended to see themselves, literally or metaphorically, as God's "Chosen People," a people uniquely favoured by circumstance to create a new, dynamic, and virtuous society. Each nation has had a very different sense of its own position in the world. As Louis Halle has said, "The Russians have always been aware of their weakness and their danger; the Americans have, since an early date, been aware of their strength and their safety ... The Russians have regarded the outside world with awe, and have felt their own points of inferiority; the Americans have regarded the outside world without respect, and have gloried in their superior way of life."[35]

These contrasting national experiences weigh heavily on the way in which each side perceives, relates to, and negotiates with the other. They are approaching present problems from quite different historical directions. One nation has been weak and is trying desperately to become strong; the other nation, which has a history of strength, has suddenly been made vulnerable and is forced to cope, for the first time, with permanent insecurity. These dissimilar pasts, and for Americans the clash between the past and present, do nothing to facilitate fruitful communication and mutual understanding. Halle has proposed that "If the Russians have been shaped by a record of failure, the Americans have been shaped by a record of success," and he wonders if this heritage of success threatens "to be the undoing of the Americans."[36] Certainly it could be, in a variety of ways: by discouraging a prudent sense of the limits of power; by overemphasizing the virtues of the unilateral pursuit of security, of going it alone; by fostering the sort of complacency and self-satisfaction that causes resentment abroad and thus militates against the working out of common objectives and co-operative planning. One gets a sense of how America appears to Moscow, when the overtly antagonistic language is dropped, from a revealing remark made in 1981 by Georgi Arbatov, the director of the Moscow Institute for the study of the United States and Canada. "I often think," he wrote, "that Americans have had unheard-of luck throughout their history, perhaps too much luck so that they cannot understand or have deep sympathy for people whose own history has been much less fortunate."[37]

In alluding to the trouble-ridden history of America's chief rival, we return, once again, to the element of fear, whose role in the making of modern Russia has been properly highlighted by Louis Halle:

> From the beginning in the ninth century, and even today, the prime driving force in Russia has been fear. Fear, rather than ambition, is the principal reason for the organization and expansion of the Russian society. Fear, rather than ambition itself, has been the great driving force. The Russians as we know them today have experienced ten centuries of constant, mortal fear. This has not been a disarming experience. It has not been an experience calculated to produce a simple, open, innocent, and guileless society.[38]

This "insecurity of political existence within the vastness of Eurasia," as another author puts it, has been a crucial legacy for the Soviet Union.[39] And as Halle further observes, "The basic factor in producing this national sense of insecurity has been geographical. Throughout its history Russia has been without natural frontiers to serve for its defense."[40] Whereas the early Americans found themselves in a large continent that was only lightly inhabited – there was, as a result, comparatively little resistance to their expansion from coast to coast – the Russians were engaged in frequent struggles with the armies of hostile neighbours. (The Americans' neighbours have been few and weak, and thus U.S. borders could remain undefended.) Such a history of struggle has been much more conducive to the growth of state power than to the flourishing of individual freedom. Survival has had to come first. The Russian craving for security in a harsh and chaotic world has certainly contributed to the emergence and consolidation of a centralized, order-imposing, autocratic government; and the widely felt fear of disorder has fostered appreciation for the rule of a strong hand, an appreciation that Western observers have often detected today among ordinary Soviet citizens. In their continuing search for security, the rulers of the state, both before and since the Revolution, have sought to push their borders outwards to more defensible positions. And in doing so they have subjected many non-Russian peoples to what now is, essentially, Russian rule. These are mostly peoples whose lands have served in the past as passageways for attacks from the West – attacks that the recent Soviet leadership has been determined not to see repeated. The present result of these bloody political struggles is that a heavy apparatus of coercion hangs over many non-Russian neighbours of Russia, that many of the citizens of these client states acquiesce only outwardly and resentfully to Soviet power, and that the Soviet leadership finds itself having to rule largely without the support of ideological consensus, without, that is, any significant degree of political legitimacy. And thus, though somewhat different in character, Russia's fundamental insecurities persist.

These various reflections on Russian history and culture, in a book on the nuclear age, are intended in part as a reminder of how one-sided so much Western commentary on the Soviet Union is, how contaminated it often is by the assumptions of Cold War modes of thought, and how inadequate our understanding tends to be of how the world looks from Moscow's point of view (which is not to say, of course, that this view has to be fully accepted or condoned). All the talk that we hear of Russian might and military capability threatens to conceal from our view a reality of at least equal importance: the insecurities and frustrations of the Soviet leadership and the anxieties that many Soviet citizens feel in the face of Western power. For the West is dynamic in a way that Russia is not. It constantly generates new ideas and new technology; it is continually thrusting into new frontiers. In certain ways the USSR is still a backward nation – antiquated, even stagnant, in certain respects – and at least some members of its ruling class know that this is so. It is the West, not the USSR, that is setting the pace and the standards in most fields of human endeavour, most obviously, perhaps, in high technology. These developments have caused considerable concern in Moscow that the "correlation of forces" is now developing unfavourably for socialism and that a resurgent West has struck much more aggressive postures in its rediscovered confrontation with the Soviet presence. Such feelings of insecurity were certainly heightened by the rhetoric and policies that were sponsored by the American government in the early 1980s, which left the Kremlin more than a little bruised. In September 1983 Stanley Hoffmann wrote of "the Soviet conviction that the Reagan Administration has adopted a relentless, coherent strategy aimed at obtaining nuclear superiority, at waging ideological, political, and economic warfare";[41] and a number of independent Western observers who visited the Soviet Union at this time were agreed that the most prominent feelings they encountered were those of fear, alarm, vulnerability – and no small amount of anger and resentment. As Seweryn Bialer observed in early 1984, Soviet leaders are not only aware of many of their nation's weaknesses, they also know that "both their friends and their adversaries fully appreciate how vulnerable they are." And one of the main reasons for this vulnerability is that "the inadequate Soviet economic machinery can barely support the costs of modernity and global ambition."[42] In short, on the global stage of competitive power politics, the Soviet Union is at some serious disadvantage.

These Soviet weaknesses, which have recently come to be more widely recognized, have been seen in certain circles as comforting and gratifying. But others argue – correctly, I think – that these weaknesses are in fact a potential source of danger for us all, especially when combined with an American policy that stresses assertiveness, toughness, and displays of muscularity. For whatever may happen, it is certain that the Kremlin will not remain passive in the face of these developments. It will fight back, as it always has in the past. It will become more defiant. It will come to put even more emphasis on vigilance, centralized discipline, and ideological orthodoxy; and it will appeal even more, in support of its demands for renewed exertions from its subjects, to those deeply rooted and widespread feelings of Russian patriotism. A kind of fortress mentality will reassert itself. It is interesting to note that a recent essay entitled "Do Soviet Leaders Test New Presidents?" finds that it is more often a new American administration that challenges the Kremlin, with results that, in the end, are usually not to U.S. liking. "For the available evidence strongly suggests," writes George Breslauer, "that U.S. efforts to seize the initiative during presidential transitions typically facilitated the efforts of Soviet hard-liners to seize the initiative in the internal political game." He thinks that "belligerent U.S. behavior at crucial turning points in Soviet politics and policy typically was followed by a Soviet hard-line ascendancy in defense policy."[43] Now, in a renewed Cold War era, as the Soviet leadership searches for ways to deal with the United States and its own internal problems, there is a danger that the strategies of its hard-liners may triumph over those of its moderates and pragmatists. The Soviet state may feel forced to gird its loins for the emerging struggle, and if it does so, the neo-Stalinist strands in its politics will be strengthened and the voices of those who are ideologically less rigid will be muted and stifled.

There is, in the mid-1980s, considerable evidence that this process of constriction is well under way. Seweryn Bialer, who visited the Soviet Union three times during the thirteen months up to January 1984, found there an angry and hostile mood. "President Reagan's rhetoric has badly shaken the self-esteem and patriotic pride of the Soviet political elites. The administration's self-righteous moralistic tone, its reduction of Soviet achievements to crimes by international outlaws from an 'evil empire' – such language stunned and humiliated the Soviet leaders." These men, he concluded, "believe that President Reagan is determined to deny the Soviet Union nothing less than its legitimacy and status as a global power. This status, they thought, had been conceded once and for all by Reagan's predecessors, not to speak of America's allies. They believe President Reagan would deny them the respect and international influence due them as an inevitable consequence of what they see as the most important accomplishment in their post-revolutionary history – the achievement of military parity with the West." As a result of this anger and humiliation, "The higher officials of the Party and government leaders have been stirred to defiant hostility toward the United States; the combination of American insult and pressure since 1982 has been made more bitter by the recognition among Russian elites of their own political and economic vulnerability. An increasingly intolerant neo-Stalinism in domestic affairs coexists with urgent advocacy of economic reform. These different tendencies share one volatile ingredient – the desire to reassert Soviet greatness at home and abroad." In short, "A rekindled sense of insecurity – insecurity that is both indigenously rooted and aggravated by the policies of its chief rival – "fires an angry and defiant response, a desire to lash out, to reassert self-esteem, to restore the diminished respect of others."[44] It should have surprised no one that throughout 1984 the Soviet leadership, in its determination not to appear weak in the face of perceived provocations, refused almost all opportunities for co-operation with the West.

All this should remind us of the dangers of pushing too hard, of talking too toughly, of causing any great power to feel humiliated. As one observer has aptly remarked, "Cold War rhetoric is open-ended – lots of accelerator, not much brake or steering wheel."[45] The Soviet leadership has rarely backed down in the face of American threats or threatening talk; instead, it has usually become more obstinate and less accommodating. It has been just as anxious to avoid policies that might appear to resemble "appeasement" as have politicians in Washington. (The aftermath of Russia's most prominent retreat, during the Cuban missile crisis, included the ousting from power of the relatively moderate Nikita Khrushchev and a massive Soviet buildup of nuclear missiles.) As the *New York Times* of 25 May 1983 correctly stated, in an editorial opposing the development of the MX missile, "Throughout the history of the nuclear arms race, the Russians have answered new American weapons not with concessions but with new Soviet weapons." The Soviet leaders, like the leaders of most great powers, have shown that they respect force and firmness, and that they are entirely capable of political compromise. But they have not responded favourably to what they have seen as intimidation from outside. This fact is well known to many Western observers of Soviet behaviour, including some who can be in no way suspected of being soft on Communism. Russia, as Dimitri Simes has pointed out, has "tended to pull together and play tough when pushed around. The Reagan Administration," he suggested in mid-1982 – and the same could be said of any U.S. government – "would be wise to encourage moderation rather than belligerence in the behavior of America's principal rival."[46] Moderation in Moscow is dependent on moderation in Washington; if the latter is lacking, any sort of productive communication is likely to break down, as it did from the late 1970s. "It is in American interests," thinks Simes, "to force the Soviets to respect U.S. military power and will. It is not in American interests to create panic in Moscow."[47] Or, as Stanley Hoffmann has put it, "Nothing could be more dangerous than giving the Soviet Union the sense of being cornered – surrounded by hostile forces masterminded by us."[48] Some commentators in 1984 were wondering if the groundwork for such dangerous developments had, perhaps, already been laid. Seweryn Bialer reported that "Reagan's challenge to the Soviet Union and the recognition by the Soviet leaders of their own vulnerability do not combine to reinforce caution in Soviet international conduct. On the contrary, in my opinion, this combination could lead Soviet policy makers to take higher risks" – and to seek further opportunities for "national self-assertion."[49] Russian nationalism and pride, it might be recalled, are at least as weighty as the nationalism and pride of the United States.

As we consider the current state of world politics, what should most alarm us, in my view, is not Soviet power *per se* – that should be taken as a given in the global theatre of sovereign states – but rather the dangerous combination of Soviet vulnerability *and* Soviet military might, a combination made very much worse by inept American diplomacy and a hopelessly simple-minded bipolar view of international affairs. It is this political admixture of strengths, weaknesses, and ideological rigidities, set in a vastly over-armed environment, that threatens to give rise to incautious actions, or miscalculations, or desperate gambles. There is, in the nuclear age, a potentially high price to pay for confrontational politics. Better ways have to be sought to work with and live with the Soviet Union, not new ways to coerce it. Attempts at coercion have consistently reinforced those orthodoxies in the USSR that are most rigid and uncompromising; those orthodoxies, in other words, that are especially threatening to Western security and least disposed to pursue the path of negotiation and coexistence. The United States has treated the Soviet Union with disdain, hatred, condescension, and fear, but rarely with respect (which is what Russians particularly want). This has been a mistake that must be remedied if the world's future is to be prudently managed.

The Soviet Union is not monolithic. It embraces a certain variety of political opinion, competition among numerous interest groups, much ethnic diversity, and a tension between inward- and outward-looking views of the world. Its citizens, like those of other countries, have their own distinctive human faces, a humanity that is often submerged under the weight of Cold War premises and stereotypes. In the hard world of international politics, no doubt firmness, strength, and resolve will always be highly valued and of the first importance in determining the character of relations between states. But if these muscular virtues are to be properly managed and not push us into the now ever-present abyss, they need to be tempered by gentler dispositions, by qualities that are related to sympathetic understanding. Of course, merely to start speaking in these tones is to cause embarrassment in certain hard-headed political circles. But perhaps more sentiment of this sort would do us no harm. As the Oxford scholar of military affairs Michael

Howard has said of Western leaders (and no doubt the same could be said of their Eastern counterparts), "they need to show a quality in which they have hitherto been notably deficient: *compassion*, the capacity to see the world through the eyes of others, even through those of our adversaries."[50] Here, certainly, is one precondition for relations governed by greater civility and less belligerence, and thus, surely, a more secure world.

Fragile Controls

During the past few years, the spate of writing concerning nuclear weapons has given rise to a small mountain of publications, and as one sifts through this miscellaneous body of literature – journalistic and scholarly, polemical and technical, humanistic and "strategic" – one finds that a small number of books stand out and warrant special attention. These are the relatively rare works that compel us to see the circumstances of our nuclear predicament in a rather different, and decidedly clearer, light. Such substantial contributions can emerge from almost any academic discipline. Paul Bracken, the author of *The Command and Control of Nuclear Forces* (Yale University Press 1983), is a political scientist and student of management. His book is rather austerely written. Its tone is cool and restrained. Its perspective is "scientific," its reasoning careful and well informed. And it bears a message of considerable importance that deeply concerns whether or not we can avoid stumbling into nuclear war.

Bracken is primarily intent on trying to explain what is likely to happen to the nuclear forces of both superpowers during a political crisis. Given such a crisis – and one can imagine hosts of possibilities, in Europe, in the Middle East, perhaps elsewhere – how would the military forces on both sides be likely to respond? How would they be put on alert? How would these mutual alerts interact to raise the level of tension? Could the process of increasing alerts be properly controlled? And if war were to break out somewhere, would it be possible to know what was actually happening, to judge the combat environment judiciously, and to control the conduct of battle? In many ways Bracken's book is rooted in commonsensical perceptions of reality. We know that large numbers of nuclear weapons exist. Anything that exists must be managed in some way. This management must be done according to certain rules and procedures. And since those things being managed could conceivably be used some day, there must be plans for using them and organizations responsible for carrying out these plans. Of course, these plans have never been tested. They exist only on paper. They are purely theoretical. But what if some day, for whatever reason, theory started to be put into practice? What would probably occur? And, in particular, could these occurrences be adequately controlled by duly authorized human hands?

In the early years of the nuclear age, before ballistic missiles appeared, questions of this sort were rarely, if ever, raised. Military planners during the 1950s were mostly concerned to ensure that they received adequate warning of attack and remained able to retaliate with massive destructiveness. Consequently, their planning requirements were modest. But by the 1960s priorities were changing. Two new "requirements" came to the head of the military agenda: first, the need to apply nuclear force in limited amounts (sometimes known as the strategy of "flexible response" or "escalation control"); and second, the need to preserve centralized political control over whatever application of force did occur. The emphasis, then, was on the need for control, the need to be able to use all sorts of weapons, including nuclear weapons, in selective, restrained, and limited ways. And the purpose of such control was to be able to fight and, in some significant way, win a nuclear war, at least in the sense of emerging as the dominant power in any post-nuclear-war world. This policy, as we saw in chapter one, remains very much in effect today.

Bracken's book is largely concerned to investigate the credibility of this policy. And what he shows, in a careful and methodical manner, is that this policy is based largely on illusion, untested assumptions, and confused thinking. It is a policy that assumes a steady flow of accurate information, but in a crisis there is almost sure to be the sort of information glut that overwhelms rational decision-making. It is a policy that assumes the continuation of intelligence-gathering; but if war were actually to begin, the channels of communication and the means of assessing what is going on are sure to be seriously disrupted, thereby preventing political leaders from arriving at informed decisions. The organizational and technical networks that, in theory, allow for the coherent direction of nuclear forces are, in fact, extremely fragile. Rendering a nuclear power partly blind, deaf, and mute would not be all that difficult (this is sometimes known as "nuclear decapitation"); and a military force that suffers from such handicaps is obviously not well placed to exercise restrained, well-managed, and discriminating action.[51] Present policy, in short, could be undermined in a multitude of ways: by the vulnerability of satellites, by the breakdown of computers, by the destruction of command centres, and by the necessity for fallible humans to make momentous decisions in very short periods of time (perhaps fifteen minutes or less). As Bracken says at one point, "We know of no literature that shows how an American president would be able to absorb warning information, assess the battlefield nuclear situation in Europe, including strikes on the Soviet Union with NATO aircraft and missiles, monitor damage inflicted on the United States, and simultaneously plan a retaliatory response – all in the space of twenty to thirty minutes. Not only are the communication and computation obstacles overwhelming, but the human aspect of the situation defies comprehension."[52]

It is clear that real power, at a time of crisis, is virtually certain to move away from political leaders and into the hands of military commanders. The chances of preserving central political control of the machinery of warfare are poor. Control is very likely to become decentralized, partly because the technology of centralized command will be in great disarray, partly because of the delegation of authority to local commanders that will take place during a crisis. What one is most likely to observe, then, is not control but chaos: a political environment in which military men, many of whom will be commanding nuclear weapons, are on their own, acting more or less independently, and mostly ignorant, as everyone else will be, of the larger pattern of events. Political judgment, in such circumstances, is very likely to be – indeed, will have to be – almost completely cast aside.

These problems are at their worst in Europe. For there nuclear and conventional weapons are intimately interconnected. Nuclear weapons are deeply integrated into the war-fighting strategies for the so-called European theatre, strategies that tend to blur the distinction between nuclear and conventional weapons. At a time of crisis the early use of at least a few nuclear weapons is a very real possibility. Even putting them on alert would involve grave risks of uncontrollable escalation, given the probable response of the other side with alerts of its own. The momentum towards war might well become virtually unstoppable. This process of a political crisis causing a military alert, which causes a momentum of military mobilization, might be tough to control, as Bracken points out in his representation of an all-too plausible scenario:

it is not all that difficult to envision a political crisis leading to an alert, and the alerting process escalating until NATO was forced to disperse its nuclear weapons from their storage positions or until conventional attacks were authorized against Soviet or U.S. submarines patrolling near enemy coasts. It is also possible to imagine a mutual alerting process reaching the point where interference or direct attack of satellites was undertaken, or where spontaneous evacuation of Soviet and American cities would occur for civil defense reasons. Few people would disagree that operating nuclear forces at such high states of alert in this environment could easily tip over into preemptive attacks and all-out war. Each nation might not want war but might feel driven to hit first rather than second. Instead of war versus peace, the decision would be seen as either striking first or striking second.[53]

As for the West's political leaders – who, in NATO, speak different languages, live in different capitals, and have different interests – it is hard to conceive how they could possibly find time to consult together, to be properly briefed, to judge wisely, and to keep control of their military subordinates. As Bracken remarks, "if a war occurs it is likely to be intrinsically uncontrollable because the NATO command system has not been designed to provide such control."[54] The existing system, in fact, is best suited, not for controlling conflict, but rather for triggering an all-out nuclear war. This, indeed, is a major source of the widespread disquiet about NATO's nuclear doctrines and what they imply. "One of the reasons for the intensity of the current debate in Europe about nuclear armaments," suggests Bracken, "is that the authorities really don't have any good answers to give to the critics. The nuclear freeze movement and other groups are asking questions for which no one has an answer, and they are consequently making many officials extremely uneasy."[55]

It seems likely, then, that the existing plans for the rational management of nuclear weapons are based largely on pure faith, and perhaps a hefty dose of wishful thinking. This is not a healthy state of affairs, partly because, as Desmond Ball has observed with regard to American strategy, while the principles of restraint and discrimination supposedly built into these plans are almost sure to be chimerical, "The danger is that ... policy-makers could well become so bemused with the sophistication of current US nuclear war plans as to believe that they could in fact control the employment of US strategic nuclear weapons in accordance with those plans."[56] This judgment is in line with the conclusions of Bracken's book. "While nuclear strategies have been getting more complicated," he writes, "the ability to carry out *any* of these strategies has been declining, because the necessary system of command and control has not been constructed. It has not been built because no one has any idea how to build it. Instead, an ever-widening chasm [has developed] between strategic ideas and the command structure's ability to carry them out."[57] The fundamental problem of the unmanageability of nuclear weapons has not been solved. Claims that these weapons are now being rationally managed are ill-founded, unconvincing, and incompatible with realistic political analysis. But however implausible the plans and doctrines may be, the systems themselves are very much in place: systems that are vast in scale, highly integrated, and extraordinarily complex, ready to be placed on hair-trigger alert. "In broadest terms," says Bracken, "the danger facing the world is that the superpowers have institutionalized a major nuclear showdown. They have built the most complex technological apparatus ever conceived, without thinking through its purpose or how to control it."[58] Here, certainly, is one of the most pressing dilemmas of contemporary existence.

In raising these issues our attention is drawn to one further point: a consideration concerning the way in which war is most likely to start. For despite all the talk about war resulting from "aggression," it is probable that, should another major war break out, it will happen more or less unintentionally, as a result of miscalculation, or diplomatic bungling, or hasty action under pressure – as a result, in short, of the inability to manage a political crisis successfully. The fear of aggression, and clumsy efforts to forestall a feared aggression, are much more likely to cause war than is aggression itself. As Bernard Brodie once observed, we "know from history that where there is enough tension, war can break out without its truly being willed by either side."[59] This is what happened in 1914. When relations between states are tense, and when at least two great powers have invested their prestige in some regional conflict, the failure to resolve the dispute, and the disinclination of either side to back down once substantial prestige is at stake, are liable to draw the contending parties closer and closer towards a direct confrontation. And the momentum of such a crisis, in which each side judges that the risks of standing firm are less hazardous than the risks of yielding, will be in danger of escaping human control, as events start to run away with those who are ostensibly in charge of them.

Resisting the drift to war in such circumstances is never easy, and today, with the ever-present nuclear threat, successful crisis management is even more demanding. "Technological progress," wrote Brodie in 1959, "is pushing us rapidly and inexorably toward a position of almost intolerable mutual menace."[60] This mutual menace is now even greater than it was a generation ago, as each side proceeds to develop weapons that the other side fears might allow it to obtain a first-strike capability (the United States is moving further in this direction than the Soviet Union). And one of the main dangers of this elaboration of a first-strike technology is that it might, in some future crisis, give rise to a pre-emptive strike by the side that feared it was about to be attacked – a strike that would probably be justified on the grounds that war had become inevitable, and that striking first would be less bad than striking second. In certain circumstances, then, taking the nuclear initiative could seem like the least of a number of evils. This danger has been explicitly addressed by Paul Warnke, former director of the u.s. Arms Control and Disarmament Agency, with reference to Soviet fears of American first-strike capabilities. If Soviet leaders, he says, "feel that we may strike first and deprive them of the ability to retaliate, then a nuclear war could start, not because of any rational calculation of advantage but because of desperation, fear, and panic."[61]

Such anxieties are likely to be greatly exacerbated by the time pressures that technology imposes on modern political decision-making. That precious commodity, time – time for reflection, time for assessment, time for communication and negotiation – is, as Alastair Buchan pointed out some years ago, "something which technical progress has been steadily eroding for a century ... Technology has steadily robbed states of that element of time and warning which they took for granted when military force moved only at marching pace."[62] With the speed of modern technology, the prospects for the exercise of sound political judgment in times of tension have become more and more problematical. We are threatened, then, not only by the destructive power of nuclear technology, but also by the velocity of events and the consequent acute pressures that decision-makers are bound to experience. Perhaps the prudent course of action, given that we can foresee the likelihood of such a frenzied situation arising some day, would be to take steps now to construct facilities for cooling crises, for slowing down the rush of events, and for finding ways to minimize misunderstandings, misreadings of intention, and misperceptions in great power relations. The dangers in failing to do so, in failing to anticipate the politics of crisis management, have been well discerned by John Keegan, an astute observer of military affairs:

> if we don't find some way of explaining ourselves across the nuclear frontier, a crisis is going to come which even the good people won't be able to steer by hand and the hot line, when misunderstandings will proliferate, menaces accumulate, and men desperate for some sure response to events will start to catch events on the wing and try to match them with the pictures in the drill book [i.e., with pre-set operational plans]. Once that starts to happen, it cannot be long before a head of government finds himself with the word "Fire" ringing in his ears and his hand on the oven door. And then it won't only be the cat that will get roasted.[63]

Positive Steps

Analysis and interpretation are important, but it is also vital to look ahead and to consider what might be done to repair past damage and to act more intelligently in the future. Looking backward, we have been concerned to inject some historical sensitivity, a degree of historical depth, into our understanding of present political circumstances. But we also want to look forward and, with an eye on the past, bring forth proposals for change that are sensible, realistic, and likely to command widespread assent. What, then, are some of the conditions that will have to be satisfied if we are to enjoy a more secure future? And what are some of the steps that could and should be taken to reduce the prospect of nuclear devastation?

First, it is vital that nations come to recognize, and to act upon, their shared interest in survival. Security cannot be achieved through unilateral action. It cannot arise out of efforts by each superpower to aggravate the other superpower's insecurity. Each side must be prepared to grant the other side the same degree of security that it seeks for itself. Indeed, each has a self-interest in seeing that the other side feels more secure. In the nuclear age national security must be based on

the pursuit of common security; it can be achieved only by working
with other states, not against them. Some measure of positive
collaboration, informed by a realistic recognition of power and
common objectives, is essential. As former U.S. Secretary of State
Cyrus Vance wrote in 1982,

> Neither the United States nor the Soviet Union can provide for its own
> security against nuclear holocaust unless it also helps to provide that
> security for the other. Neither can seek a decisive nuclear advantage
> without the risk of provoking an attack in which both would be destroyed.
>
> In short, the most basic security of all for the superpowers –
> security from nuclear war – cannot in the final analysis be dominated
> by competition. Their security must be based on an unparalleled
> degree of cooperation.[64]

Total security cannot be achieved and should not be sought, least of all
through unilateral measures – that is, the attempt, which is now
completely misguided, to save ourselves by ourselves. "There is only
one way the United States and the Soviet Union can save themselves
from each other's missiles," as Thomas Powers has remarked, "and
that is together."[65]

Second, in order to highlight this mutuality of interest, this common
stake in survival, it will be imperative to reduce the adversarial
character of the relationship between the world's two dominant
powers. The U.S.-Soviet rivalry is bound to continue. It is a rivalry
that has deep structural and cultural roots. But it is vital that this
competition be managed prudently, that it not be allowed to pro-
voke a direct confrontation, and that the nuclear dimension of the
rivalry be greatly reduced. The common interest in avoiding nuclear
catastrophe should take precedence over all other considerations. This
means that, in an effort to ease tensions and build on common interests,
there must be a revival of diplomacy and of non-military communications of all sorts. Economic, cultural, and scientific exchanges should
be actively promoted and expanded. Rather than accentuating the sore
points and aggravations of the East-West relationship, there is a
pressing need to normalize this relationship as much as possible and to
rescue it from at least some of the paralysis of Cold War confrontational premises, including much of the gratuitous emphasis on antagonistic
relations that is embedded in the orthodoxies of deterrence. Each side

is inordinately afraid of "appeasing" its adversary and prefers to be seen as tough. But toughness can be costly. For while, as a writer on military affairs once observed, a crude policy of appeasement "never pays, the mutual friction of two 'tough' policies generates a shower of sparks, and any of these are liable to detonate an explosion."[66] Flexibility is not a sign of weakness. It is essential both to co-operate and to deter; but thus far political energies have been devoted almost entirely to the latter.

It has become increasingly apparent, in this world of science and technology, that we all inhabit one small, rather fragile, interdependent world; in such a world the deliberate attempt to keep one powerful state very much at arm's length, and perhaps even to isolate it, makes no sense at all. As the *New York Times* put it in September 1983, just after a Soviet fighter shot down a Korean airliner, "You do not make Moscow more accountable by drumming it out of the world community."[67] Of course, Moscow would have to make its own accommodations; and all the evidence from the past indicates that it is most likely to do so, that its reformist and more flexible and least xenophobic tendencies are most likely to thrive, when it is not being menacingly challenged by the West. In this pursuit of a less adversarial relationship, arms control has an important role to play, partly as a builder of mutual confidence and trust, and thus of more cordial political relations. "Limitation of armaments will not end war," as Hanson Baldwin pointed out in 1947, "for armaments are not the primary cause of war, but rather surface evidence of an infection in the body politic. But excessive armaments encourage an armaments race, breed fear and insecurity and add to the multiple frictions which bring on war."[68] The process of limiting and perhaps reducing the means of destruction probably cannot get seriously under way unless a modicum of warmth and civility is restored to the u.s.-Soviet relationship, and this will require the curtailing of the ideological shouting match that has so often taken place between those in charge of the world's most deadly military arsenals. If such self-restraint can come about, arms control is more likely to advance and in turn make its own contribution to a healthier international politics and a reduction of mutual fears.

Third, more people must realize that nuclear weapons have no military utility. They are, in fact, unusable, or, if used, they are probably suicidal. In a nuclear war, after the darkness lifts, the ancient distinction between victor and vanquished is likely to be meaningless.

To depend so heavily on such useless weapons for our security, then, is fundamentally irrational. Many prominent men have come to this conclusion, including Field Marshall Lord Carver, former chief of the British defence staff; Admiral Noel Gayler, former commander in chief of U.S. forces in the Pacific; Lord Zuckerman, former chief science adviser to the British government; and Robert McNamara, former U.S. secretary of defense. The late Earl Mountbatten, one of Britain's most distinguished leaders of this century, in 1979 expressed his view as follows: "As a military man who has given half a century of active service I say in all sincerity that the nuclear arms race has no military purpose. Wars cannot be fought with nuclear weapons. Their existence only adds to our perils because of the illusions which they have generated."[69]

Nuclear weapons, then, are means without any appropriate ends; and the use of these weapons has no credibility as an instrument of policy. It is especially vital that these propositions come to be accepted by growing numbers of the military: men and women who are able to see that opposition to nuclear weapons is entirely compatible with patriotism, loyalty, and professional honour. The physicist Freeman Dyson has pointed to the importance of such a to-be-hoped-for military change of heart:

We need above all to have sound and realistic military doctrines – doctrines that make clear that the actual use of nuclear weapons cannot either defend our country or defend our allies, that the actual use of nuclear weapons in a world of great powers armed with thousands of warheads cannot serve any sane military purpose whatsoever. If our military doctrines and plans once recognize these facts, then our military leaders and those of our allies and adversaries may be able to agree upon practical measures to make the world safer for all of us. If our soldiers once understand that they cannot defend us with nuclear weapons, then they may contribute their great moral and political influence to helping us create a world in which non-nuclear defense is possible. If the soldiers can once be turned against nuclear weapons, then ordinary civilians and politicians will be able to campaign for nuclear disarmament without being considered cowardly or unpatriotic. The road of discipline and patriotic self-sacrifice need no longer be the road to nuclear holocaust.[70]

There can be little doubt, I think, that an anti-nuclear alliance that brings together both military and civilian constituencies is likely to be much more successful than a civilian peace movement that confronts an overwhelmingly hostile military establishment, an establishment which, despite objections that it has been unable to answer, is still deeply attached to its plans for the conduct of nuclear warfare.

Fourth, the nuclear arms race can be brought under some degree of rational control only if the weapons laboratories and their backers can be firmly restrained. As long as military scientists are encouraged to invent and design as they please, whatever the human and political costs, and as long as the world's various military establishments are passionately committed to elaborate programs for the "weaponizing" of new advances in scientific knowledge, there is little hope for effective arms control, much less substantial disarmament. Progress will be possible only if arms control agreements are able to impose constraints on both military science and the bureaucratic constituencies that have a vested interest in keeping this science on a fast track. Appropriate restraints might be pursued in various ways: perhaps by means of a comprehensive nuclear test ban treaty (this might well be the single most important step that could be taken to curtail the arms race); perhaps by limiting the facilities for producing plutonium and enriched uranium; perhaps by prohibiting the testing of certain kinds of new weaponry (most testing can be readily monitored by other parties), such as the testing of all weapons designed for use in outer space. These practical steps are, at present, easily within our means, given the political will. It would be generally desirable as well if military research were directed away from the development of the means of destruction, where it is now heavily concentrated, and increasingly towards those kinds of technology that are related to (and compatible with) improvements in monitoring, surveillance, and confidence-building. No doubt there are many techniques and scientific avenues that could be fruitfully explored. But whatever methods might prove most promising, the prime objective should be to reimpose political control over technological drift; that is, to bring technology closer in line with rational human ends.

Fifth, along with these long-term endeavours, it will also be necessary to invest much more heavily in collaborative efforts for the successful management of political crises. This is a pressing problem. We have seen how fragile the operational systems of the nuclear superpowers are and how vulnerable and agitated they are likely to be at a time of serious political tension. There is a grave danger, in the present environment of highly integrated military technologies, short response times, and potential hair-trigger alerts, that diplomatic paralysis might lead to a loss of political control of the course of events. It is in such circumstances that fear and panic are most likely to predominate, and then the chances greatly increase that one side will start to think seriously about a pre-emptive strike, and that field commanders will be allowed greater scope for independent military action. It is vital to take steps now to facilitate the handling of such dangerous situations. One possible practical step is the establishment of jointly manned crisis and communications centres, which would be especially charged with clarifying intentions and dispositions and with minimizing the risks of misperceptions and miscalculations. John Keegan has alluded to the potential benefits of such a facility. He asks whether "what we really need for a secure world is ... to create a sort of bi-partisan situation room in which the velocities of crisis could be brought back under control by the mutual evaluation of common intelligence reports and the exposition of the intended, rather than perceived, significance of governmental responses."[71] Certainly, anything that served to buy more time and to reinvigorate diplomacy at times of high tension would be a positive step towards avoiding war.

Whatever practical arrangements might prove most feasible, the fundamental objective would be to preserve stability in the course of a crisis, to prevent it from getting out of hand and triggering a disastrous course of events that all parties actually wanted not to occur. There may be other practical measures as well that warrant serious consideration, such as easing the time pressures on both sides' decision-makers by pulling back those weapons that can strike very quickly at major command centres. Wisdom, in this respect, indicates that both Pershing IIs in West Germany and Soviet submarine-launched missiles near the U.S. Atlantic coast, with their short flight times, are to nobody's benefit. Mutual agreements for withdrawing such missiles, along with other hard-headed agreements based on the recognition that squeezing the other fellow too hard only increases the risk of mutual destruction, would contribute to the prospects for keeping a lid on the political pot when the pot threatens to boil over, as it most certainly will someday. The need, in short, is to construct much more sturdy buffers: buffers between, on the one hand, the frenzy that crises always generate and, on the other hand, the world's actual capacity for self-annihilation.

Sixth and finally, some unilateral initiative of restraint is needed to break the current log-jam, and that initiative, in my view, can best come from the United States. This initiative could take the form of a withdrawal of all battlefield nuclear weapons from Europe; or a declaration of no-first-use of nuclear weapons; or a moratorium on the deployment of sea-launched cruise missiles; or a freeze on the number of warheads for long-range delivery systems (present u.s. plans call for a substantial increase in the number of "strategic" warheads). Better still, such an initiative could embrace an unconditional, unilateral reduction in the American inventory of nuclear warheads by, say, 10 or 15 per cent, with an invitation to the Soviet Union to do the same. Soviet leaders would have a strong self-interest in reciprocating, if only because the arms race is a much heavier burden on the Russian economy than it is on that of the United States. Once the process of limiting and reducing nuclear weapons is under way, the mutuality of disarming would be likely to develop its own momentum. But some nation has to take the first step. The United States is better suited to this role, partly because, as Herbert York, a long-time American defence specialist, has said of his country,

> we are richer and more powerful ... our science and technology are more dynamic ... [and] we generate more ideas of all kinds. For these very reasons, we can and must take the lead in cooling the arms race ... in inducing the rest of the world to move in the direction of arms control, disarmament and sanity.
>
> Just as our unilateral actions were in large part responsible for the current dangerous state of affairs, we must expect that unilateral moves on our part will be necessary if we are ever to get the whole process reversed.[72]

These words were written in 1970. Since then the unilateral actions of both sides have, with rare exceptions, concerned the buildup, not the reduction, of nuclear arsenals.

Thought and Language

We inhabit a peculiar world. In the search for what is called national security, the great powers pursue an arms race that is virtually guaranteed to heighten insecurity, as it has since the late 1940s. In Western political cultures there is much agitated talk of the "Soviet threat," and yet many – perhaps most – of the actual problems we confront, both domestically and globally, have little or nothing to do with the USSR. One notices that most of the bloody conflicts of the early 1980s were largely or entirely unrelated to Soviet initiatives (Afghanistan is the sole significant exception). All this talk about "the threat" (in the Soviet Union the threat is said to come from "capitalist imperialism") serves, it is clear, not to explain the world, but rather to deflect our attention from a much more fundamental and common threat: the massive presence in the world of nuclear weaponry and the extent to which this weaponry has become deeply embedded in our system of international relations. The everyday language of political opportunism, especially the Cold War language from both sides of the great-power divide, is designed in part to obscure the reality of this peril and to present an invariably one-sided view of the East-West confrontation as the central drama of the modern world. In the course of these power and propaganda struggles, much mystification is deployed, which the mass media, as a rule, obediently disseminate. One's own side's nuclear arsenal is made to appear, by a kind of linguistic sleight of hand, as benign as possible: the other side is said to "threaten" and is at all time a "potential aggressor"; we, it is said, merely "deter" and prepare to act in self-defence.[73] Of course, the rhetoric of peace continues to be dispensed at least as liberally as ever before, and meanwhile the militarization of international relations and the increasing refinement of the technologies of destruction actively proceed apace.

In attempting to dispel some of the mists that enshroud our perceptions of these present dangers, all of us, no doubt, can make our own particular contributions. But however we might choose to direct our energies, it will be necessary at all times to address the fundamental issue of language – the issue that George Orwell, and others, have been so acutely aware of. For much of the language of conventional politics is a barrier to clear thinking and critical understanding. It is riddled with stereotypes; it is often (as in *1984*) deliberately dishonest; it is consciously reworked and reshaped by powerful interests to discourage awkward questions and to help put people's minds at ease. A sensitivity to language is almost always the beginning of political wisdom – never more so than in the nuclear age. It is clear, certainly, that much of the orthodox language of nuclear strategists and military specialists is long overdue for close inspection. The preoccupation of these people is overwhelmingly with technique, with the means to achieve presupposed ends; the ends themselves, the purposes of policies, are seldom scrutinized, and it is just such purposes that warrant, and would benefit from, critical attention. Moreover, the world of these nuclear experts and professional strategists is alarmingly simplistic and lacking in nuance. They are intolerant of ambiguity. For them "enemies" and "aggressors" are easy to identify and "threats" are conceived almost exclusively in military terms; and their notion of "security" is so remarkably constricted that they exclude from consideration most of what human security actually means and has meant in most civilizations. This lack of subtlety, this narrowing of vision, and this warping of language should not go unchallenged. Finally, it is important to recognize how much of the specialist literature on the nuclear age is decidedly ethnocentric. It is vitiated by a persistent failure to imagine, sympathetically, alternative views of the world (including those of supposed enemies); by an inability to accord any degree of legitimacy to adversaries' views of their own security; and by a chronic tendency to equate national self-interest with universal values.[74] Such ethnocentrism is, of course, by no means novel. But it is now much more dangerous in its implications. Never before has the potential price been so high for failing to understand how others see the world. And here, again, many of us can contribute to a broader discussion, especially by challenging those stereotyping images of outsiders that ethnocentrism always promotes, and by resisting the contaminating influences of narrow, parochial, and confrontational modes of thought.

In this global arena of claims and counter-claims, of rapidly changing "friends" and "enemies," of newly perceived "threats" and officially designated "vital interests," of military jargon and theoretical formulations about human conflict that are devoid of common sense, perhaps we would do best to begin our critical scrutiny of life in the nuclear age with language itself. For language, as the late Arthur Koestler once observed, is not only man's principal intellectual resource, it is also our "deadliest weapon" and, "in view of its explosive emotive potentials, a constant threat to survival."[75] People are killed in words many times over before they die from bombs. Here, perhaps, in the means through which we understand ourselves and perceive outsiders – in our created language – is the first real threat that needs to be disciplined, civilized, treated with care – and at least partly disarmed.

Epilogue

"We must remember," wrote a prominent actor in the politics of the nuclear age, "that the advancement of science and technology can be like a whip, cracking over our heads, encouraging us to spend more and more money on national security. We can always build better rockets or better bombs tomorrow than the ones we have today. But the goal of accumulating the very latest weapons in sufficient quantity to be completely safe, once and for all – that goal is an illusion, a dream."[1] The author of these words, Nikita S. Khrushchev, had a rather mixed and not entirely edifying record of political conduct. But in his retirement, with time for reflection, Khrushchev's gifts for a certain intuitive understanding of the processes of world affairs became more clearly evident, as in this remark on the acute military-technological pressures of our age. These pressures have grown with time. The search for assured security is never-ceasing and yet the goal is never attained. And as this search proceeds, in the hope that our new condition of assured vulnerability can be somehow reversed and overcome, new technical fixes are proposed, new military technologies are promoted, and the path to a safer future is repeatedly said to depend on a policy of "peace through strength," in which strength is defined largely in military terms. But this policy has not produced happy results. "Improvements" in military technology have resulted in a precipitous decline in global security.

Khrushchev's warning was remarkably akin to that delivered by President Dwight D. Eisenhower in his farewell address to the nation in January 1961, when he cautioned his listeners about the mighty and perhaps overbearing presence in the American body politic of the military-industrial complex. He spoke of how the "conjunction of an immense military establishment and a large arms industry is new in the American experience," and how, "In the councils of government, we must guard against the acquisition of unwarranted influence" by these new institutional forces. "The potential for the disastrous rise of misplaced power exists and will persist." He then went on to remark on how "the sweeping changes in our industrial-military posture" were largely a result of "the technological revolution during recent decades," and he warned that "we must also be alert to the ... danger that public policy could itself become the captive of a scientific-technological elite."[2] The very different experiences of these two old warriors and politicians appear to have led them to rather similar conclusions. And the thrust of their departing words serves, I think, to direct our attention to a central core of concerns: to the formidable strength of the military dynamic in modern society, to the imposing weight that military science exerts in public life, and to the very dubious benefits that modern military technologies have afforded their users as they persist in their search for national security.

The nuclear age has witnessed not only the sudden appearance of weapons of mass destruction. It has witnessed as well the emergence of the national security state, a form of state power that depends, fundamentally, on military definitions of existence. In the United States the national security state has very much acquired a life of its own. It has helped to create and sustain a very powerful presidency. It has also, as Daniel Yergin observes, "turned legions of 'private' companies into permanent clients of the Defense Department. Of course," he adds, "the national security state does not exist apart from other realities. It has grown, in part, dialectically with the 'total security state' of the Soviet Union."[3] The world's various national security establishments have been actively involved in the fostering of militarized modes of thought and conduct and assumptions about the world. "Security" has come to be construed pre-eminently in relation to military force. People have been encouraged to see a rival society as largely the sum of its tanks, missiles, warheads, megatonnage, and presumed evil intentions. These developments are testimonies to the failure of modern diplomacy and, as E.P. Thompson has put it, "the relegation of diplomacy to an annex of the military system."[4] Certainly, the revival of diplomacy, as a political priority of the highest order, will be essential if this stark and unyielding militarization of relations among states is to be in any way resisted and reduced. The political agenda will have to be overhauled and reshaped to accord better with the inescapable realities of our own technological creations. "Generals can make war," as Freeman Dyson reminds us, "but it takes a diplomat to make peace. Great diplomats are rarer than great generals. Throughout human history the tools of war have been studied too much and the tools of diplomacy too little. In the modern era, more than ever before, weaponry commands disproportionate attention, and the art of understanding the purposes of foreign governments is neglected."[5] Diplomacy, in short, must be reinvigorated as a vital counterweight to the frenetic search for military solutions to political problems.

If the national security state has come to take on a life of its own, so too has that systemic culture of miscommunication that we know as the Cold War. Indeed – and this is fairly obvious – it is the perpetuation of the Cold War that critically sustains the vitality of this huge apparatus of state security. References are made, time and time again, to "the threat" in order to justify new military initiatives and the enlargement of some agency of state power. The complexities of world affairs are persistently presented in terms of "them" and "us," of aggression and freedom, of political differences that are said to be irreconcilable. And yet, the question that ought to be asked and pondered at length – the question that deserves to have priority in political discourse much more often than it has heretofore – is this: What is this Cold War now about? For as one examines the actual differences between East and West, and the interests that divide them, one cannot help but notice that, compared with the hostilities between great powers in the past, the contentious issues between the United States and the Soviet Union are not all that remarkable. This peculiarity of u.s.-Soviet relations was noticed in 1981 by the editorial writers of *The Times* of London, who argued that

> The huge accumulations of weaponry which the two brandish at each other are wholly out of proportion to any genuine conflict of interests. There is no serious competition for essential resources, or for territory that is truly vital to the security of either, and the ideological fires have dwindled on both sides. In strictly objective terms a reasonable degree of accommodation should be easily attainable. But many

114

conflicts throughout history have been essentially irrational, and it is with this irrationality that we have to deal. The emperors may have no clothes but they are quite capable of destroying each other and everyone around them.[6]

(Remarkably, having offered this sensible assessment, the editorialists immediately reversed their standpoint and went on to say: "But that is as far as the analogy goes. One emperor is on our side and the other is not." Such a sudden descent in the quality of political thinking is, perhaps, a symptom of the intellectual malaise that results from the constrictions and rigidities of Cold War modes of perception.)

The antagonisms of the Cold War are now, in many respects, sustained by a deep inertia. They are capable of reproducing themselves and resisting pressures for accommodation and restraint. The Cold War has produced its own language, its own sustaining assumptions, its own narrow ways of looking at global relations. Its modes of thinking penetrate much of modern culture, in both East and West. Ideological hostility works actively, and usually successfully, to preserve those tensions that give "national security" establishments their reason for existence. In some nations these military-scientific-bureaucratic elites are now so powerful that they have become virtual laws unto themselves, substantially detached from any effective democratic accountability. The presence of nuclear weapons in the arsenals of the two greatest of these states serves to reinforce East-West fissures, to heighten fears and anxieties, and to undermine the search for workable political accords and modes of co-existence. Nuclear weaponry not only threatens to blow us all up, it also threatens, by its massive and looming presence and because of the vested interests that cling to it, to nip in the bud and effectively stifle any gestures of reconciliation, or signs of restraint, or any disposition to substitute diplomacy for military clout. Nuclear arsenals have been central components of this Cold War polarization. And arms and ideology have fuelled each other's fires. "The Cold War," according to E.P. Thompson, "has become a habit, an addiction. But it is a habit supported by very powerful material interests in each bloc." He suggests that "the military and the security services and their political servants *need* the Cold War. They have a direct interest in its continuance." "What is the Cold War now about?" he asks, "It is about itself."[7]

Let us leave the last word on this matter to a man of distinguished intellect and rich political experience, the diplomat and historian George F. Kennan. In 1976 Kennan offered the following remarks on the nuclear dimension of the relationship between the Soviet Union and the United States – remarks that convey more solid intelligence than volumes of technical studies by strategists and military analysts:

> The fears and other reactions engendered by this nuclear rivalry have now become a factor in our relations with Russia of far greater importance than the underlying ideological and political differences. The real conflicts of interest and outlook, for all their seriousness, are limited ones. There is nothing in them that could not yield to patience, change, and a readiness for accommodation. There is nothing in them, above all, that could really be solved by – and, therefore, nothing that could justify – a major war, let alone the sort of global cataclysm that seems to pre-empt so many of our plans and discussions. Yet this fact is constantly being crowded out of our consciousness by the prominence, and the misleading implications, of the military competition. An image arises, if only initially for purposes of military planning, of an utterly inhuman adversary, committed to our total destruction, and committed to it not for any coherent political reason but only because he has the capacity to inflict it. This unreal image presents itself to both parties; and in the name of a response to it whole great economies are distorted, whole populations are to some extent impoverished, vast amounts of productive capacity needed for constructive purposes in a troubled world are devoted to sterile and destructive ones; a proliferation of nuclear weaponry is encouraged and pursued that only increases with every day the dimensions and dangers of the problem to which it is supposed to be responsive; and the true nature of our relations with the Soviet Union and its peoples becomes obscured and distorted by the cloud of anxieties and panicky assumptions that falls across its face. The nuclear rivalry, in other words, begins to ride along of its own momentum, like an object in space, divorced from any cause or rationale other than the fears it engenders, corrupting and distorting a relationship that, while not devoid of serious problems, never needed to be one of mortal antagonism.[8]

Reason, clearly, demands that in the interest of mutual survival we back off from this militarized posturing, learn to nourish the commonality that underlies our experiences, and embark on policies that will promote the *de*nuclearization of relations among nation states. Reason also suggests that we shall have to question the rationale of warfare itself. For the potential impact of modern weaponry is so staggering, and the implications of its use so frightening and pervasive, that the whole enterprise of fighting wars now cries out for re-examination. Is it possible that war is becoming politically obsolete? It may well be that its days are numbered. But even if it comes to pass that peoples do, indeed, lose confidence in the utility of warfare, how are disputes to be resolved henceforth? Given that war, in the past, has been the final resort in human struggles, and given the unprecedented peril that it now poses, shall we be able to find alternatives to war, ways of managing discord and conflicts of interest and of reconciling rivals to each other's existence without putting life itself totally in jeopardy?

"As geological time is reckoned," observed Bertrand Russell in the mid-1950s, "Man has so far existed only for a very short period ... What he has achieved, especially during the last 6,000 years, is something utterly new in the history of the Cosmos, so far at least as we are acquainted with it. For countless ages the sun rose and set, the moon waxed and waned, the stars shone in the night, but it was only with the coming of Man that these things were understood ... In art and literature and religion," he continued, "some men have shown a sublimity of feeling which makes the species worth preserving. Is all this to end in trivial horror because so few men are able to think of Man rather than of this or that group of men? Is our race so destitute of wisdom, so incapable of impartial love, so blind even to the simplest dictates of self-preservation, that the last proof of its ... cleverness is to be the termination of all life on our planet?"[9] Russell's questions have not lost their pertinence. Nor will they ever, as long as human beings exist. For having eaten of the tree of knowledge, having grasped some of nature's essential truths, we have made for ourselves a new state of nature with which we shall always have to live.

A Guide
to Further
Reading

Too much of what has been written about the nuclear age falls into two narrow categories. There has been, on the one hand, the literature of protest. These are works that have decried the arms race, warned of the apocalypse, and called for a revolutionary change in human thinking. Some of this writing has been of value, but it has suffered, on the whole, from both a surfeit of engagement and insufficient detachment, and a consequent inattentiveness to the task of trying to understand how the nuclear age has taken shape: inattentiveness, in short, to the need to think historically, in order both to understand and to act effectively. Such partisan writing, even when perceptive and properly critical, is too liable to simplify reality, gloss over difficult issues, and depreciate the hard job of explanation. On the other hand, there is the literature produced by the so-called defence intellectuals, most of whom are concerned with what they call "strategic studies." These are persons who, as a rule, are closely associated with various state security establishments. They are heavily committed to military definitions of reality, their political outlooks are usually constricted, and most of their thinking is strongly conditioned by Cold War viewpoints and assumptions. Some of them engage in theorizing of very questionable utility, and others design rationales to justify the purchase of whatever new military technologies are emerging. This, too, is largely partisan writing, although its style of expression is in the techno-rational mode.

To understand the nuclear age one has to go beyond these two traditions and seek out other works – works that are reasonably even-handed, not completely presentist, and historically sensitive. It is this historical dimension that requires particular emphasis. For the public debates about nuclear issues have been left, for the most part, in the hands of non-historians. This is regrettable and, increasingly, indefensible. The nuclear age cries out for serious scrutiny from a historical perspective – a perspective that is essential both in helping us to grasp the complexities of our present circumstances and in contributing to future actions and decisions that, it is to be hoped, might better serve the cause of survival and improved international relations. Now, with the advantage of greater historical distance, and with the release of much new documentation on the post-war period, it is certainly possible to gain a much better appreciation of the dynamics of the arms race and the impact of nuclear weapons on modern culture and global relations. Good books and articles are available for study. New works of originality continue to appear. The intention of this guide is to draw attention to some of the most enlightening readings that bear on our presence in the nuclear age, in particular, those that are properly conscious of the past and of our constant need to enlarge and deepen our memories.

You don't have to know much physics to deal with the human dimensions of the nuclear age, but it doesn't hurt to know a little. Lucid and brief accounts of basic nuclear physics are offered in Walter C. Patterson, *Nuclear Power* (1976, pb), the first half of chap. 1; and Margaret Gowing, *Independence and Deterrence: Britain and Atomic Energy, 1945–1952*, vol. 1 (1974), 451–64. For commendably clear discussions of the major developments in nuclear physics during the years before the Second World War, see C.P. Snow, *The Physicists* (1981), chaps 1–6; and Margaret Gowing, *Britain and Atomic Energy, 1939–1945* (1964), 3–30. Some useful details are also available in Robert Jungk, *Brighter than a Thousand Suns: A Personal History of the Atomic Scientists* (1958, pb), chaps 1–5. During the 1930s research and teaching in physics became inescapably caught up in international politics, notably the rise of fascism. For a good representation of the momentous upheavals in Nazi Germany, see Alan D. Beyerchen, *Scientists under Hitler: Politics and the Physics Community in the Third Reich* (1977, pb), especially chaps 1–3; and on the emigration of scores of physicists from fascist Europe, most of whom ended up in the United States, see Charles Weiner, "A New Site for the Seminar: The Refugees and American Physics in the Thirties," in Donald Fleming and Bernard Bailyn, eds, *The Intellectual Migration: Europe and America, 1930–1960* (1969), 190–228; and Gerald Holton, "The Migration of Physicists to the United States," *Bulletin of the Atomic Scientists*, April 1984, 18–24. The crucial discoveries of 1938–9 in atomic physics, and their political implications, are competently outlined in Ronald W. Clark, *The Greatest Power on Earth: The International Race for Nuclear Supremacy* (1980), chap. 3.

The developments in atomic physics and weaponry during the Second World War may be examined through a number of admirable studies. On activities involving Britain the authoritative history is Margaret Gowing's *Britain and Atomic Energy 1939–1945* (1964), which is broader in scope than the title suggests, since it includes discussions of work in Canada and the United States. The comparable official history on the United States during these years of war is Richard G. Hewlett and Oscar E. Anderson, Jr, *The New World, 1939/46: A History of the United States Atomic Energy Commission*, vol. 1 (1962), chaps 1–11. The involvement of the physics profession in the design and production of American armaments is concisely recounted in Daniel J. Kevles, *The Physicists: The History of a Scientific Community in Modern America* (1978, pb), chaps 19–21. Under the auspices of what came to be known as the Manhattan Project, the first atomic bombs were manufactured in the seclusion of Los Alamos, New Mexico in 1943–5. The work of this scientific hothouse and intensely creative society is remembered by a number of its members in Lawrence Badash, Joseph O. Hirschfelder, and Herbert P. Broida, eds, *Reminiscences of Los Alamos, 1943–1945* (1980, pb); and Jane Wilson, ed., *All in Our Time: The Reminiscences of Twelve Nuclear Pioneers* (1975, pb), chaps 7–12. Robert Oppenheimer, the scientific director at Los Alamos, is the subject of an evocative biography by Peter Goodchild, *J. Robert Oppenhiemer, 'Shatterer of Worlds'* (1980; 1984 pb edn. entitled *Oppenheimer: The Father of the Bomb*). The initiatives and influence of another prominent physicist are examined by Carol S. Gruber, "Manhattan Project Maverick: The Case of Leo Szilard," *Prologue: Journal of the National Archives* 15, no. 2 (Summer 1983), 72–87. The interconnections between the birth of this new military technology and the Allied conduct of the war, up to the collapse of Nazi Germany, are perceptively examined in one of the best historical works written thus far on the nuclear age, Martin J. Sherwin, *A World Destroyed: The Atomic Bomb and the Grand*

Alliance (1975, pb), 1–140. Soviet responses to Western innovations in atomic weapons are considered in David Holloway, "Entering the Nuclear Arms Race: The Soviet Decision to Build the Atomic Bomb, 1939–45," *Social Studies of Science* 11, no. 2 (May 1981), 159–97.

The events of the spring and summer of 1945 – the policies of the Truman presidency, the decision to use the atomic bomb against Japan, the bomb's impact on Soviet-American relations – are discussed in Sherwin's *A World Destroyed*, 141–238. The thinking behind the bombings of Japan is the subject of a useful selection of readings and documents edited by Barton J. Bernstein, *The Atomic Bomb: The Critical Issues* (1976, pb). See also Bernstein's *Hiroshima and Nagasaki Reconsidered: The Atomic Bombings of Japan and the Origins of the Cold War, 1941–1945* (booklet, 1975); and Robert L. Messer, *The End of an Alliance: James F. Byrnes, Roosevelt, Truman, and the Origins of the Cold War* (1982), 84–119. Alice Kimball Smith, *A Peril and a Hope: The Scientists' Movement in America, 1945–47* (1965, pb), chap. 1, discusses some of the opposition to the bomb's use. For a debate on the justifications for these bombings, see Joseph Alsop and David Joravsky, "Was the Hiroshima Bomb Necessary? An Exchange," *New York Review of Books*, 23 October 1980, 37–42, with further comments in the issue of 19 February 1981, 44–5. The three bombs completed before mid-August 1945 were used on 16 July (in the Alamogordo desert, New Mexico), 6 August (on Hiroshima), and 9 August (on Nagasaki). There is now a considerable literature on the destruction of Hiroshima and Nagasaki. John Hersey's *Hiroshima* (1946, pb) was one of the first Western accounts of the devastation and is still worth reading. First-hand observations by Japanese survivors in the two cities include Michihiko Hachiya, *Hiroshima Diary: The Journal of a Japanese Physician, August 6-September 30, 1945* (1955, pb); Arata Osada, ed., *Children of the A-Bomb: The Testament of the Boys and Girls of Hiroshima* (1963); and Tatsuichiro Akizuki, *Nagasaki 1945* (1981, pb). Japan Broadcasting Corporation, ed., *Unforgettable Fire: Pictures Drawn by Atomic Bomb Survivors* (1977, pb) presents vivid visual testimonies as to how the bombing of Hiroshima was experienced and later remembered. The most detailed, comprehensive, and up-to-date report on the impact, both immediate and long term, of the two atomic bombings is the study by the Committee for the Compilation of Materials on Damage Caused by the Atomic Bombs in Hiroshima and Nagasaki, *Hiroshima and Nagasaki:*

The Physical, Medical, and Social Effects of the Atomic Bombings (1982, pb). For a psychological study of Hiroshima's victims who survived, see Robert Jay Lifton, *Death in Life: Survivors of Hiroshima* (1967, pb).

Serious studies of atomic weapons during the years immediately after the Second World War are now appearing, of which the most notable is Gregg Herken, *The Winning Weapon: The Atomic Bomb in the Cold War 1945–1950* (1980, pb). A concise treatment of some of the main themes of Herken's book is provided in his article "'A Most Deadly Illusion': The Atomic Secret and American Nuclear Weapons Policy, 1945–1950," *Pacific Historical Review* 49 (1980), 51–76. See also Larry G. Gerber, "The Baruch Plan and the Origins of the Cold War," *Diplomatic History* 6, no. 1 (Winter 1982), 69–95; and chaps 12–17 of Hewlett and Anderson, *The New World, 1939/1946.* A number of the earliest attempts to understand the implications of atomic weapons are still worth reading. See, in particular, Bernard Brodie, ed., *The Absolute Weapon: Atomic Power and World Order* (1946); Jacob Viner, "The Implications of the Atomic Bomb for International Relations," *Proceedings of the American Philosophical Society* 90 (1946), 53–8; Dexter Masters and Katharine Way, eds, *One World or None* (1946); and, for recent accounts of the earliest instances of strategic nuclear thinking, Fred Kaplan, *The Wizards of Armageddon* (1983), chaps 1–3, and Lawrence Freedman, *The Evolution of Nuclear Strategy* (1981, pb), chaps 1–4. James Eayrs, *In Defence of Canada: Peacemaking and Deterrence* (1972, pb), chap. 5, discusses Canadian policies and objectives concerning atomic energy during the 1940s and Canada's responses to American and British actions.

The U.S. government, it now appears, became committed shortly after the Second World War to a policy of preserving its exclusive control of atomic energy technology as long as possible and of maximizing the political advantages of its monopoly. Despite the expectations of most knowledgeable scientists that the USSR could and would manufacture its own bombs within five years, numerous political and military leaders predicted that U.S. industrial-technological superiority, combined with inadequate Soviet supplies of fissionable material, would ensure American hegemony for a very long time. Consequently, the testing of the first Soviet atomic bomb in August 1949 was greeted in many circles with shock, dismay, and trepidation. During the ten months after this Soviet test, which witnessed the triumph of Mao's forces in China and a debate over whether or not to develop the hydrogen bomb and concluded with the outbreak of war in Korea, there were several major developments in the intensification of the nuclear arms race and the Cold War. For accounts of this period, see Richard G. Hewlett and Francis Duncan, *Atomic Shield: A History of the United States Atomic Energy Commission, volume II, 1947/1952* (1972, pb), chaps 12 and 13; Herken, *Winning Weapon*, chaps 14 and 15; Herbert F. York, *The Advisors: Oppenheimer, Teller, and the Superbomb* (1976), chap. 4; Freedman, *Evolution of Nuclear Strategy*, chap. 5; David Alan Rosenberg, "American Atomic Strategy and the Hydrogen Bomb Decision," *Journal of American History* 66, no. 1 (June 1979), 62–87; and Barton J. Bernstein, "Truman and the H-bomb," *Bulletin of the Atomic Scientists*, March 1984, 12–18. The political context of these times (1949–50) is well outlined in Samuel F. Wells, "Sounding the Tocsin: NSC 68 and the Soviet Threat," *International Security* 4, no. 2 (Fall 1979), especially 116–39; and John Lewis Gaddis, *Strategies of Containment: A Critical Appraisal of Postwar American National Security Policy* (1982, pb), chap. 4. McGeorge Bundy has also reflected on the events of this period: see his "The Missed Chance to Stop the H-Bomb," *New York Review of Books*, 13 May 1982, 13–22. The principal authority on post-war developments in Britain is Margaret Gowing, *Independence and Deterrence: Britain and Atomic Energy, 1945–1952* (2 vols, 1974).

While the beginnings of the nuclear age can now be studied in some depth and with a certain sense of perspective, the same cannot be said as unreservedly of the period since the early 1950s. A great deal has been written about nuclear weapons, but much of it is the product of particular ideological debates, bureaucratic infighting, and national anxieties at particular moments of time. These various records (memoirs, speeches, political commentary, articulated military doctrine, declassified government documents, and the like) comprise an important part of the documentation on the nuclear age. However, they have (for the most part) yet to be carefully sifted, critically scrutinized, and situated within the political contexts from which they arose. Serious interpretive studies, then, are still thin on the ground, although some valuable work had been recently published. The most systematic and judicious studies that relate to the past three decades are Freedman's *Evolution of Nuclear Strategy*, which focuses on changes in military doctrine; and Gaddis's *Strategies of Containment*, especially chaps. 5–7 and parts of chaps 9 and 10, which considers the role of nuclear weapons in U.S. foreign policy from Eisenhower on. Both books include ample notes and good, up-to-date bibliographies. The most perceptive commentator on military strategy during this generation was Bernard Brodie; see especially various chapters in his *Strategy in the Missile Age* (1959) and *War and Politics* (1973, pb).

Introductory accounts of the arms race since the Second World War are available in Thomas B. Larson, *Soviet-American Rivalry* (1978, pb), 167–216 and 273–7, and Richard J. Barnet, *The Giants: Russia and America* (1977, pb), chap. 5. For a dissident Marxist view of the arms race, which challenges much Western conventional wisdom, see Roy Medvedev and Zhores Medvedev, "The USSR and the Arms Race," *New Left Review*, no. 130 (November/December 1981), 5–22. American developments during the 1950s – doctrinal, political, and military – are the subject of Freedman's *Evolution of Nuclear Strategy*, chaps 6 and 9–11; Gaddis's *Strategies of Containment*, chaps 5 and 6; and Jerome H. Kahan, *Security in the Nuclear Age: Developing U.S. Strategic Arms Policy* (1975), chap. 1. There is much useful information and commentary concerning nuclear issues in Stephen E. Ambrose, *Eisenhower, Vol Two: The President* (1984). See also Samuel F. Wells, Jr, "The Origins of Massive Retaliation," *Political Science Quarterly* 96, no. 1 (Spring 1981), 31–52. The most satisfactory, concise accounts of the 1960s are in Freedman, *Evolution of Nuclear Strategy*, chaps 15–17, and Gaddis, *Strategies of Containment*, chap. 7. For an admirable monographic study of part of this decade, see Desmond Ball, *Politics and Force Levels: The Strategic Missile Program of the Kennedy Administration* (1980). Jerome H. Kahan and Anne K. Long, "The Cuban Missile Crisis: A Study of Its Strategic Context," *Political Science Quarterly* 87, no. 4 (December 1972), 564–90, discusses both the immediate background to the Soviet initiatives in Cuba and the long-term acceleration of the Soviet arms buildup that occurred after 1962. See also Barton J. Bernstein, "The Cuban Missile Crisis," in Lynn H. Miller and Ronald W. Pruessen, eds, *Reflections on the Cold War: A Quarter Century of American Foreign Policy* (1974), 108–42, and Robin Edmonds, *Soviet Foreign Policy: The Brezhnev Years* (1983, pb), 23–37. Nuclear strategy since the later 1960s is discussed in Freedman, *Evolution of Nuclear Strategy*, chaps 22–5. For a short, even-handed account of the 1960s and 1970s, see Stephen A. Garrett, "Detente and the Military Balance," *Bulletin of the Atomic Scientists* 33, no. 4 (April 1977), 10–20. Public opinion during these years is thoughtfully examined in Paul Boyer, "From Activism to Apathy: The American People and Nuclear Weapons, 1963–1980," *Journal of American History* 70, no. 4 (March 1984), 821–44.

Any attempt to understand the very recent and present realities of nuclear weaponry encounter numerous difficulties. Much propaganda is put out, by the political and military authorities in many countries, and what is not obviously propagandistic is commonly misleading, or mystifying, or contaminated by the simplistic political formulations of Cold War rhetoric. A great deal of writing in this field is sponsored, directly or in various indirect ways, by military and national security establishments, which consequently play a large role in setting the agendas for scholarly inquiry, thereby helping to ensure that only certain questions are actively pursued, that awkward evidence receives little publicity, and that inconvenient hypotheses remain unexplored. This literature is also characterized by much juggling of numbers, which can be done in all sorts of polemically creative ways. Indeed, statistical misrepresentations and (in particular) the removing of numerical calculations from their broader contexts are endemic to the field. Moreover, much pertinent information is classified and thus unavailable for public scrutiny, although whether this "hidden factor" matters much for an understanding of the essential dynamics of the nuclear arms race is a moot point. It does, however, increase the likelihood of media-manipulation by means of politically inspired leaks. In the Soviet Union there is virtually no open discussion of nuclear issues. Party organs promulgate predictable dogma and self-righteous doctrinal declarations, and most of the basic information about Soviet nuclear strategy and weapons capabilities is kept under tight wraps (at least from Soviet citizens; the United States has many sophisticated means of intelligence gathering). This penchant for secrecy has frequently encouraged Western military analysts to assume the worst about the might and intentions of the Soviet state. (In reality, secrecy in the USSR has often been intended to conceal from the outside world the actual fragility and deficiencies of Soviet power.)

How, then, might one proceed in trying to understand what is now going on? One approach is to read works that are informed by different assumptions about the world. Two recent books offer such a contrast.

Living with Nuclear Weapons, by the Harvard Nuclear Study Group (1983, pb), outlines what could be broadly regarded as the American mainstream position (which differs somewhat from that of the Reagan administration), and it states its case in a clear, informative, straightforward manner. This work is the best introduction to the conventional wisdom about nuclear weaponry. For a significantly different analysis, from a European perspective, see Gwyn Prins, ed., *Defended to Death: A Study of the Nuclear Arms Race from the Cambridge Disarmament Seminar* (1983, pb), which provides a thoughtful and well-informed account of the dynamics of the arms race and summary statements of many of the current arguments concerning the utility (or non-utility) of nuclear weaponry. Another introductory study of value is offered by Bruce Russett, *The Prisoners of Insecurity: Nuclear Deterrence, the Arms Race, and Arms Control* (1983, pb). David N. Schwartz, *NATO's Nuclear Dilemmas* (1983, pb), is a historically oriented account of the presence of nuclear weapons in Europe. See also two works by David Holloway: "Nuclear Weapons in Europe," *Bulletin of the Atomic Scientists*, April 1983, 17–24; and *The Soviet Union and the Arms Race* (1983, pb), chap. 4. Some useful reflections on contemporary world affairs have been presented by the Israeli diplomat Abba Eban in his book *The New Diplomacy: International Affairs in the Modern Age* (1983), especially chaps 1–3 and 8. *Common Security: A Programme for Disarmament*, by the Palme Commission (1982, pb), both examines the current state of international relations and offers concrete proposals for reform.

What about the Russians? This question is often asked and not always easy to answer. Happily, one can now learn a great deal from David Holloway's *The Soviet Union and the Arms Race*, which is exceptionally well informed, judicious, and even-handed. Holloway's principal objective is to understand Soviet policy, not to condemn or defend it, and he succeeds admirably. See also Robert P. Berman and John C. Baker, *Soviet Strategic Forces: Requirements and Responses* (1982, pb), especially chap. 3. The following articles cast much useful light on Soviet thinking about nuclear weapons: John Erickson, "The Soviet View of Deterrence: A General Survey," *Survival* (published by the International Institute for Strategic Studies) 24, no. 6 (November/December 1982), 242–51; two articles by Raymond L. Garthoff, "Mutual Deterrence, Parity and Strategic Arms Limitation in Soviet Policy," in Derek Leebaert, ed., *Soviet Military Thinking* (1981),

92–124, and "The Soviet Military and SALT," in John Baylis and Gerald Segal, eds, *Soviet Strategy* (1981), 154–82; and Robert L. Arnett, "Soviet Attitudes towards Nuclear War: Do They Really Think They Can Win?" in Baylis and Segal, eds 55–74. Soviet actions in Europe are thoughtfully examined in Raymond Garthoff, "The Soviet ss–20 Decision," *Survival*, May/June 1983, 110–19. Concise and perceptive surveys of Soviet military and foreign policy are available in David R. Jones, "Russian Tradition and Soviet Military Policy," *Current History*, May 1983, 197–200 and 230–2; Ken Booth, "The Military Instrument in Soviet Foreign Policy," in Baylis and Segal, eds, *Soviet Strategy*, 75–101; Alexander Dallin, "The Soviet Union: The Making of Foreign Policy," *Bulletin of the Atomic Scientists*, August/September 1983, 27–31; Robert G. Kaiser, *Russia: The People and the Power* (1976, pb), chap. 12; and various chapters of Robin Edmonds, *Soviet Foreign Policy: The Brezhnev Years* (1983, pb). There is much acute commentary in the various writings of George F. Kennan; see especially his book, *The Nuclear Delusion: Soviet-American Relations in the Atomic Age* (1983,pb). Robert H. Johnson, "Periods of Peril: The Window of Vulnerability and Other Myths," *Foreign Affairs* 61, no. 4 (Spring 1983), 950–70, discusses the history of American assessments of "the Soviet threat."

While material of substance concerning the nuclear age can now be found in a wide range of publications, several sources are of particular importance. *International Security*, which is a quarterly, and the *Bulletin of the Atomic Scientists*, which appears ten times a year, deserve a regular reading. See also the various publications of two of the leading research centres in the field: the International Institute for Strategic Studies in London, whose publications include a bimonthly, *Survival*, and a series of occasional papers known as the *Adelphi Papers*; and the Stockholm International Peace Research Institute, which publishes, among various titles, the annual guide, *World Armaments and Disarmament*. Sheila Tobias, et al., *What Kinds of Guns Are They Buying for Your Butter? A Beginner's Guide to Defense, Weaponry, and Military Spending* (1982; pb edn. entitled *The People's Guide to National Defense*), is a useful primer on the American military establishment, broadly conceived. Thomas B. Cochran, William M. Arkin, and Milton M. Hoenig, *Nuclear Weapons Databook, Volume I: U.S. Nuclear Forces and Capabilities* (1984, pb), is an invaluable reference work, which also includes much

historical information. It is the first book to appear in a projected
eight-volume series published under the auspices of the Natural
Resources Defence Council; later volumes are planned to cover topics
such as "Soviet Nuclear Weapons," "Arms Control," and "The History
of Nuclear Weapons." For further explanations of the nature of modern
military technology, see Kosta Tsipis, *Arsenal: Understanding
Weapons in the Nuclear Age* (1983); and for a stimulating discussion of
one of the heretofore neglected aspects of survival in the nuclear age,
see Paul Bracken, *The Command and Control of Nuclear Forces*
(1983).

Finally, a few efforts have been made to offer more broadly
conceived interpretations of the nuclear age. Michael Mandelbaum,
*The Nuclear Revolution: International Politics before and after
Hiroshima* (1981), chap. 1, is worth reading, as is Barbara Tuchman,
"The American People and Military Power in Historical Perspective,"
Adelphi Papers, no. 173 (IISS, 1982), 5–13. See also several of the
essays in E.P. Thompson, *Beyond the Cold War* (1982, pb). A
probing discussion of the various novelties of the nuclear age is
available in Hans. J. Morgenthau, "The Future of Man," chap. 3 of his
Science: Servant or Master? (1972). Two recent books of a reflective
character include many perceptive observations: Freeman Dyson,
Weapons and Hope (1984), and Jonathan Schell, *The Abolition*
(1984).

Notes

Preface

1 J.R. Oppenheimer, "Atomic Weapons," *Proceedings of the American Philosophical Society*, 90, no. 1 (January 1946): 7.
2 Hans J. Morgenthau, "The Four Paradoxes of Nuclear Strategy," *American Political Science Review*, 58 (1964): 23. See also his book, *Science: Servant or Master?* (New York: New American Library 1972), chap. 3, "The Future of Man."
3 Escott Reid, *On Duty: A Canadian at the Making of the United Nations, 1945–1946* (Toronto: McClelland and Stewart 1983), 93.

Chapter 1

1 O.R. Frisch, "Eye Witness Report of Nuclear Explosion, 16.7.45," reproduced in Margaret Gowing, *Britain and Atomic Energy 1939–1945* (London: Macmillan 1964), Appendix 5, 441.
2 William L. Laurence, *Men and Atoms: The Discovery, the Uses and the Future of Atomic Energy* (New York: Simon and Schuster 1959), 116–17.
3 "Report on the Alamogordo Bomb Test, 18 July 1945," reproduced in Martin Sherwin, *A World Destroyed: The Atomic Bomb and the Grand Alliance* (New York: Knopf 1975), 308–10.
4 Joseph Hirschfelder, "The Scientific and Technical Miracle at Los Alamos," in Lawrence Badash et al. eds, *Reminiscences of Los Alamos, 1943–1945* (Dordrecht, Holland: D. Reidel 1980), 76–7.

5 Sherwin, *World Destroyed*, 312.

6 Herbert George Wells, *The World Set Free* (London: Collins 1956; first pub. 1914), 126. Harold Nicolson, in his novel *Public Faces*, published in 1933, also imagined the discovery of nuclear bombs and the impact they would have on international relations. He set the story in 1939 and conceived a scenario in which the British government alone develops the capacity to make nuclear bombs. The climax of the narrative occurs when the British Air Ministry sets off an unauthorized demonstration explosion in the Atlantic Ocean, somewhere north of the Caribbean; it wipes out a number of ships in the area and creates great tidal waves which hit the coast of South Carolina, killing some 80,000 people. The other great powers are suitably outraged at (and terrified by) the British action. However, all ends happily, for universal fear of the new weapon becomes the basis for an international agreement on general disarmament.

7 C.P. Snow, *The Physicists* (Boston and Toronto: Little, Brown & Co. 1981), Appendix I, 176–7.

8 The most authoritative source on these bombings is *Hiroshima and Nagasaki: The Physical, Medical, and Social Effects of the Atomic Bombings*, published by the Committee for the Compilation of Materials on Damage Caused by the Atomic Bombs in Hiroshima and Nagasaki (New York: Basic Books 1981).

9 Bernard Brodie, *Strategy in the Missile Age* (Princeton, NJ: Princeton University Press 1959), 149.

10 Niels Bohr, "Science and Civilization," in Dexter Masters and Katharine Way, eds, *One World or None* (New York: McGraw-Hill 1946), ix.

11 Field Marshal Lord Carver, *A Policy for Peace* (London: Faber and Faber 1982), 13.

12 Isador Rabi, as quoted in Gregg Herken, "Mad about the Bomb," *Harper's*, December 1983, 51.

13 See, for example, the essays on "Nuclear War: The Aftermath," published in *AMBIO: A Journal of the Human Environment* 11, nos 2–3 (1982); and Carl Sagan, "Nuclear War and Climatic Catastrophe: Some Policy Implications," *Foreign Affairs* 62, no. 2 (Winter 1983/4), 257–92. Military planners, in assessing the damage likely to be caused by nuclear war, have systematically underestimated the collateral destruction (especially from fire and radiation) that would result from nuclear explosions.

14 John Keegan, "The Specter of Conventional War," *Harper's*, July 1983, 14.

15 Bernard Brodie, ed., *The Absolute Weapon: Atomic Power and World Order* (New York: Harcourt, Brace 1946), 76.

16 Colin S. Gray, "Nuclear Strategy: The Case for a Theory of Victory," *International Security* 4, no. 1 (Summer 1979), 55; and "Correspondence," *International Security* 6, no. 1 (Summer 1981), 185–6.

17 Colin S. Gray and Keith Payne, "Victory is Possible," *Foreign Policy*, no. 39 (Summer 1980), 14. Another writer, in concluding a survey of U.S. nuclear strategies, suggests that "In the years ahead, we will have to pay a great deal of attention to the problems of preparing for war – persuading the Soviets that they cannot defeat us by using nuclear weapons and preparing to achieve rational military and political objectives if deterrence fails." Progress, he thinks, "will require that we first dispel some of the notions which have tended to underpin" our emphasis on deterrence, such as the opinion "that counterforce targeting and defensive systems are inherently dangerous, that nuclear weapons cannot have military and political utility and that competition in the strategic nuclear arena is always undesirable." Aaron L. Friedberg, "A History of the U.S. Strategic 'Doctrine' – 1945 to 1980," *Journal of Strategic Studies* 3 (December 1980), 66.

18 Desmond Ball, *Can Nuclear War Be Controlled?* (London: International Institute for Strategic Studies, Adelphi Papers, no. 169, 1981), 1–2.

19 Desmond Ball, *Targeting for Strategic Deterrence* (London: International Institute for Strategic Studies, Adelphi Papers, no. 185, 1983), 23, 25, and 39–40.

20 Colin S. Gray, "Foreword" to Keith B. Payne, *Nuclear Deterrence in U.S.-Soviet Relations* (Boulder, CO: Westview Press 1982), xiv.

21 Gray, "Nuclear Strategy," 61; and Gray and Payne, "Victory is Possible," 21.

22 Richard Burt, "The Relevance of Arms Control in the 1980s," *Daedalus* 110, no. 1 (Winter 1981), 170–1.

23 Leon Sloss and Marc Dean Millot, "U.S. Nuclear Strategy in Evolution," *Strategic Review* 12, no. 1 (Winter 1984), 26–7. As an authoritative reference work has put it, "Today, policy is based on the belief that the limited use of nuclear weapons is possible. Indeed, a 'war-fighting' strategy involving nuclear weapons is seen as the only

credible deterrent." Thomas B. Cochran, William M. Arkin, and Milton M. Hoenig, *Nuclear Weapons Databook, Volume I: U.S. Nuclear Forces and Capabilities* (Cambridge, MA: Ballinger 1984), 2.

24 Admiral Gene R. LaRocque, "America's Nuclear Ferment: Opportunities for Change," *Defense Monitor* 12, no. 3 (1983), 5 (published by the Center for Defense Information, Washington, DC).

25 Allan Krass and Dan Smith, "Nuclear Strategy and Technology," in Mary Kaldor and Dan Smith, eds, *Disarming Europe* (London: Merlin Press 1982), 7.

26 Abba Eban, *The New Diplomacy: International Affairs in the Modern Age* (New York: Random House 1983), 78.

27 Barry M. Blechman and Stephen S. Kaplan, *Force without War: U.S. Armed Forces as a Political Instrument* (Washington, DC: Brookings Institution 1978), 47–9; and Desmond Ball, "U.S. Strategic Forces: How Would They Be Used?" *International Security* 7, no. 3 (Winter 1982/3), 41–3.

28 "Report of the President's Commission on Strategic Forces (Excerpts), 11 April 1983," *Survival*, July/August 1983, 177. The joint chiefs of staff's *Dictionary of Military and Associated Terms* defines deterrence as "a state of mind brought about by the existence of a credible threat of unacceptable counter action." Quoted in LaRocque, "America's Nuclear Ferment," 4–5.

29 Christoph Bertram, in his introduction to *The Future of Strategic Deterrence, Part I* (International Institute for Strategic Studies: Adelphi Papers, no. 160, 1980), 1.

30 Leon Wieseltier, *Nuclear War, Nuclear Peace* (New York: Holt, Rinehart and Winston 1983), 52.

31 LaRocque, "America's Nuclear Ferment," 5.

32 *Manchester Guardian Weekly*, 27 December 1981, 9.

33 Bernard Brodie, "The Anatomy of Deterrence," *World Politics* 11, no. 2 (January 1959), 175.

34 Hans J. Morgenthau, "The Four Paradoxes of Nuclear Strategy," *American Political Science Review* 58 (1964), 24.

35 Brodie, "Anatomy of Deterrence," 175.

36 André Fontaine, "What Weapons against War?" *Manchester Guardian Weekly*, 3 July 1983, 12.

37 Jonathan Schell, "Reflections (Nuclear Arms – Part I)," *New Yorker*, 2 January 1984, 64–5.

38 Herbert Butterfield, "Human Nature and the Dominion of Fear," in his

International Conflict in the Twentieth Century (New York: Harper 1960), 95.

39 Hanson W. Baldwin, *The Price of Power* (New York: Harper 1947), 328.

40 Jonathan Schell, "Reflections (Nuclear Arms – Part II)," *New Yorker*, 9 January 1984, 54.

41 Michael Mandelbaum, "The Bomb, Dread, and Eternity," *International Security* 5, no. 2 (Fall 1980), 20.

42 Andrew Cockburn, *The Threat: Inside the Soviet Military Machine* (New York: Random House 1983), 193.

43 Robert J. Art and Kenneth N. Waltz, eds, *The Use of Force: International Politics and Foreign Policy* (Boston: Little, Brown 1971), 4.

44 Fred Kaplan, *The Wizards of Armageddon* (New York: Simon and Schuster 1983), 390.

45 Wolfgang K.H. Panofsky, "Science, Technology and the Arms Race," *Physics Today*, June 1981, 32–3.

46 Butterfield, "Human Nature and the Dominion of Fear," 95.

47 Eban, *New Diplomacy*, 294.

Chapter 2

1 "The Franck Report, June 11, 1945," reproduced in Alice Kimball Smith, *A Peril and a Hope: The Scientists' Movement in America, 1945–47* (Cambridge, MA: MIT Press, rev. edn., 1970), 376.

2 David Holloway, "Entering the Nuclear Arms Race: The Soviet Decision to Build the Atomic Bomb, 1939–45," *Social Studies of Science* 11, no. 2 (May 1981), 184; and Holloway, *The Soviet Union and the Arms Race* (New Haven; CT: Yale University Press 1983), 20. When General Dwight Eisenhower, the Supreme Commander of the Allied Forces in Europe, heard in July 1945 of his government's plans to atom-bomb Japan he expressed his "grave misgivings, first on the basis of my belief that Japan was already defeated and that dropping the bomb was completely unnecessary, and secondly because I thought that our country should avoid shocking world opinion by the use of a weapon whose employment was, I thought, no longer mandatory as a measure to save American lives." Dwight D. Eisenhower, *The White House Years: Mandate for Change, 1953–1956* (New York: Doubleday 1963), 312–13.

A generation after Hiroshima, Nikita Khrushchev, in his unauthorized memoirs, was probably expressing genuine, widely felt Soviet fears, as well as the party line, when he recalled that "The most urgent military problem facing us after the war was the need to build nuclear weapons. We had to catch up with the Americans ... We knew that the reactionary forces of the world, led by the United States, had decided to place all their bets on nuclear weapons. We also knew that the Western imperialists were not one bit squeamish about the means they used to achieve their goal of liquidating socialism and restoring capitalism." Stalin, he asserted, saw "that the prospect of a military conflict with the United States was all too possible and not at all encouraging for our side." *Khrushchev Remembers: The Last Testament*, translated and edited by Strobe Talbott (Boston: Little, Brown 1974), 62.

3   Alexander Werth, *Russia at War 1941–1945* (London: Barrie and Rockliff 1964), 1037; see also Barton J. Bernstein, "Roosevelt, Truman, and the Atomic Bomb, 1941–1945: A Reinterpretation," *Political Science Quarterly* 90, no. 1 (Spring 1975), 66. At least one American observer, shortly after the end of the Second World War, was able to imagine how the Soviet Union must have felt. "The use of the atomic bombs in August against Japan," wrote Irving Langmuir, "must have come as a great shock. Most of the Russians probably felt that the security that they thought they had reached was suddenly ended." Dexter Masters and Katharine Way, eds, *One World or None* (New York: McGraw-Hill 1946), 50.

4   Alexis de Tocqueville, *Democracy in America*, translated by Henry Reeve (2 vols; New York 1898), vol. I, 558–9.

5   Daniel Yergin, *Shattered Peace: The Origins of the Cold War and the National Security State* (Boston: Houghton Mifflin 1977), 7.

6   See Martin J. Sherwin, "The Atomic Bomb and the Origins of the Cold War: u.s. Atomic-Energy Policy and Diplomacy, 1941–45," *American Historical Review*, 78, no. 4 (March 1973), 945–68.

7   John Swettenham, *McNaughton, volume 3: 1944–1966* (Toronto: Ryerson Press 1969), 124.

8   Gregg Herken, *The Winning Weapon: The Atomic Bomb in the Cold War 1945–1950* (New York: Knopf 1980), 170. Herken's book offers a well-documented account of the Baruch plan; see especially chaps 8 and 9. See also Richard G. Hewlett and Oscar E. Anderson, *The New World, 1939/1946: A History of the United States Atomic Energy Commission*, vol. i (University Park, PA: Pennsylvania State

University Press), chaps 15 and 16; and Larry G. Gerber, "The Baruch Plan and the Origins of the Cold War," *Diplomatic History* 6, no. 1 (Winter 1982), 69–95.

9 Herken, *Winning Weapon*, 32.

10 Much of the evidence in support of these statements is presented in Herken's book, parts one and two. See also his essay, "'A Most Deadly Illusion': The Atomic Secret and American Nuclear Weapons Policy, 1945–1950," *Pacific Historical Review*, 49 (1980), 51–76.

11 David Alan Rosenberg, "u.s. Nuclear Stockpile, 1945 to 1950," *Bulletin of the Atomic Scientists* 38, no. 5 (May 1982), 26.

12 H.H. Arnold, *Global Mission* (New York: Harper 1949), 615.

13 Senator Brien McMahon, Democrat, of Connecticut, as quoted in Robert J. Donovan, *Tumultuous Years: The Presidency of Harry S. Truman 1949–1953* (New York: Norton 1982), 101.

14 Rosenberg, "U.S. Nuclear Stockpile," 26; and the same author's "The Origins of Overkill: Nuclear Weapons and American Strategy, 1945–1960," *International Security* 7, no. 4 (Spring 1983), 23.

15 Lawrence Freedman, *The Evolution of Nuclear Strategy* (London: Macmillan 1981), 63.

16 Samuel F. Wells, Jr, "The Origins of Massive Retaliation," *Political Science Quarterly* 96, no. 1 (Spring 1981), 34.

17 Quoted in Fred Kaplan, *The Wizards of Armageddon* (New York: Simon and Schuster 1983), 183–4.

18 Wells, "Massive Retaliation," 35.

19 John Lewis Gaddis, *Strategies of Containment: A Critical Appraisal of Postwar American National Security Policy* (New York: Oxford University Press 1982), 171.

20 *Foreign Relations of the United States 1952–1954: Volume V, Western European Security, Part 1* (Washington, DC: u.s. Government, 1983), 512. See also Gaddis, *Strategies of Containment*, 149.

21 Bernard Brodie, *Strategy in the Missile Age* (Princeton, NJ: Princeton University Press 1959), 320.

22 Michael Howard, "Reassurance and Deterrence: Western Defense in the 1980s," *Foreign Affairs* 61, no. 2 (Winter 1982/83), 312.

23 Maxwell D. Taylor, *The Uncertain Trumpet* (New York: Harper 1960), 13.

24 Thomas B. Cochran, William M. Arkin, and Milton M. Hoenig, *Nuclear Weapons Databook, volume I: U.S. Nuclear Forces and Capabilities* (Cambridge, MA: Ballinger 1984), 14–15.

25   Alexander Werth, *Russia: The Post-war Years* (London: Robert Hale 1971), 302. The physicist Freeman Dyson recalls "an evening that I spent at the bar of the Bomber Command officers' mess at a time in 1944 when Britain's bombers were still suffering heavy losses in their nightly attacks on German cities. I listened then to a group of drunken headquarters staff officers discussing the routes they would order their planes to take to Leningrad and Moscow in the war with Russia which they were looking forward to after this little business in Germany was over. Oppenheimer had heard similar talk in his encounters with the American Air Force." "Reflections (Nuclear Weapons – Part III)," *New Yorker*, 20 February 1984, 69.

26   Nikolai V. Sivachev and Nikolai N. Yakolev, *Russia and the United States* (Chicago: University of Chicago Press 1979), 221–2.

27   Herken, *Winning Weapon*, 318–19; and David MacIsaac, *The Air Force and Strategic Thought, 1945–1951* (Wilson Center, Washington, DC: International Security Studies Program, Working Papers no. 8, 1979), 19–20 and 22. David Lilienthal, chairman of the Atomic Energy Commission, represented a conversation he had with Senator Brien McMahon, on 31 October 1949, as "Pretty discouraging. What he is talking [about] is the inevitability of war with the Russians, and what he says adds up to one thing: blow them off the face of the earth, quick, before they do the same to us – and we haven't much time." *The Journals of David E. Lilienthal, vol. II: The Atomic Energy Years 1945–1950* (New York: Harper and Row 1964), 584–5.

28   Ronald Steel, *Walter Lippman and the American Century* (Boston: Little, Brown 1980), 451. See also the evidence presented in Richard Ned Lebow, "Windows of Opportunity: Do States Jump through Them?" *International Security* 9, no. 1 (Summer 1984), 168–70.

29   Rosenberg, "Origins of Overkill," 33–4.

30   See the discussion and references in Ronald W. Clark, *The Life of Bertrand Russell* (New York: Knopf 1976), chap. 19. "I felt hopeful," Russell recalls in his autobiography, "when the Baruch Proposal was made by the United States to Russia. I thought better of it then, and of the American motives in making it, than I have since learned to think, but I still wish that the Russians had accepted it." Remembering his suggestion concerning the threat of nuclear war, he records that "My chief defence of the view I held in 1948 was that I thought Russia very likely to yield to the demands of the West." *The Autobiography of Bertrand Russell, volume III: 1944–1967* (London: Allen and Unwin 1969), 17–18.

31 Louis J. Halle, *The Cold War as History* (New York: Harper and Row 1967), 172–3.

32 There are thoughtful remarks on preventive nuclear war in Hanson W. Baldwin, *The Price of Power* (New York: Harper 1947), 300–2; and P.M.S. Blackett, *Atomic Weapons and East-West Relations* (Cambridge: Cambridge University Press 1956), 84–9.

33 It is said that the reason Ernest Bevin, the British Foreign Secretary, "thought it indispensable for Britain to have atomic weapons had less to do with deterrence than with his reluctance to leave the Americans in sole control: 'We could not afford to acquiesce in an American monopoly of this new development.'" (George Walden, "Capability Bevin," *London Review of Books*, 2–15 February 1984, 8). See especially Alan Bullock, *Ernest Bevin: Foreign Secretary, 1945–1951* (London: Heinemann 1983), 352–3.

34 Holloway, *Soviet Union and the Arms Race*, 24–6.

35 Kaplan, *Wizards of Armageddon*, 290.

36 *Manchester Guardian Weekly*, 15 August 1982, 9.

37 Ted Greenwood, *Making the MIRV: A Study of Defense Decision Making* (Cambridge, MA: Ballinger 1975), 95.

38 Desmond Ball, *Politics and Force Levels: The Strategic Missile Program of the Kennedy Administration* (Berkeley and Los Angeles: University of California Press 1980), 180 and 182. There is much evidence concerning the American commitment to nuclear superiority in Stephen E. Ambrose, *Eisenhower, Vol. Two: The President* (New York: Simon and Schuster, 1984).

39 Thomas S. Power, *Design for Survival* (New York: Coward-McCann 1965), 128.

40 Curtis E. LeMay, with MacKinlay Kantor, *Mission with LeMay* (Garden City, NY: Doubleday 1965), 563. "Combined with able diplomacy," LeMay wrote in a later book, "military superiority has had real success in promoting peace, particularly when that superiority rests in the hands of an intrinsically peaceful country. With an umbrella of nuclear superiority capable of fighting and winning a general war, we can employ an infinite number of lesser strategic options along the spectrum of conflict." Curtis E. LeMay, with Dale O. Smith, *America Is in Danger* (New York: Funk and Wagnalls 1968), 79.

Similar views were expressed in a book co-authored by a retired admiral: Phyllis Schlafly and Chester Ward, *Strike from Space: How the Russians May Destroy Us* (New York: Devin-Adair 1966).

"If America builds and maintains superior military strength at the top rungs of the escalation ladder," they asserted, "we need never worry about escalation, nor about defeat, nor about surrender" (178). Nuclear weapons, in their view, should be seen as a great force for good: "The unlimited nuclear power discovered and developed by America gives our nation the greatest opportunity in history to bring about world peace" (194). Those who cautioned the U.S. against a continual arms race were written off as "gravediggers."

41 Taylor, *Uncertain Trumpet*, 58–9.

42 Ball, *Politics and Force Levels*, 185.

43 Power, *Design for Survival*, 83.

44 LeMay, *America Is in Danger*, 63 and 117.

45 Jerome H. Kahan, *Security in the Nuclear Age: Developing U.S. Strategic Arms Policy* (Washington, DC: Brookings Institution 1975), 63–4.

46 *Khrushchev Remembers*, translated and edited by Strobe Talbott (Boston: Little, Brown 1970), 516–17.

47 *Khrushchev Remembers: The Last Testament* (1974), 56.

48 *Khrushchev Remembers* (1970), 494.

49 Eban, *New Diplomacy*, 120. Similarly, David Holloway suggests that "Strategic nuclear power is the clearest symbol of Soviet super-power status, and the claim to strategic parity shades into the assertion that the Soviet Union is the United States's political equal." *Soviet Union and the Arms Race*, 180.

    A pervasive theme in Khrushchev's memoirs is the Soviet craving for international recognition. He frequently expresses pride in his nation's rise to power and influence, from its previous lowly status. "It's no small thing," he writes at one point, "that we have lived to see the day when the Soviet Union is considered, in terms of its economic and military might, one of the two most powerful countries in the world." *Khrushchev Remembers: The Last Testament* (1974), 604.

50 W.R. Crocker, *Australian Ambassador* (Melbourne: Melbourne University Press 1971), 161. The United States, complained Albert Einstein in 1947, "has conducted its Russian policy as though it were convinced that fear is the greatest of all diplomatic instruments." Albert Einstein, "Atomic War or Peace," in his *Ideas and Opinions* (New York: Dell 1973; first pub. 1954), 130.

51 On Soviet fears and pessimism during the 1980s, see Lawrence T.

Caldwell and Robert Legvold, "Reagan through Soviet Eyes," *Foreign Policy*, no. 52 (Fall 1983), 3–21; and Thomas Powers, "What Is It About?" *Atlantic Monthly*, January 1984, 37–9 and 44–50.

52 John Lewis Gaddis, "Containment: Its Past and Future," *International Security* 5, no. 4 (Spring 1981), 77.

53 Halle, *Cold War as History*, 234.

54 Michael Howard, "The Edwardian Arms Race," in Donald Read, ed., *Edwardian England* (New Brunswick, NJ: Rutgers University Press 1982), 147.

55 McGeorge Bundy, in Alan F. Neidle, ed. *Nuclear Negotiations: Reassessing Arms Control Goals in U.S.-Soviet Relations* (Austin, TX: Lyndon B. Johnson School of Public Affairs 1982), 27.

56 James F. Leonard, a former U.S. disarmament ambassador, in ibid., 17.

57 The most recent study to document the serious deficiencies of the Soviet armed forces is Andrew Cockburn, *The Threat: Inside the Soviet Military Machine* (New York: Random House 1983).

58 Lawrence Freedman, *U.S. Intelligence and the Soviet Strategic Threat* (London: Macmillan 1977), 194.

59 Bernard J. O'Keefe, *Nuclear Hostages* (Boston: Houghton Mifflin 1983), 228–9. For a lucid account of the business of constructing scenarios of vulnerability, see Kaplan, *Wizards of Armageddon*. A recent example of vulnerability-panic – of the kind O'Keefe alludes to – is Keith B. Payne, *Nuclear Deterrence in U.S.-Soviet Relations* (Boulder, CO: Westview Press 1982), chap. 7.

60 For a helpful survey of exaggerated American views of Soviet power, see Robert H. Johnson, "Periods of Peril: The Window of Vulnerability and Other Myths," *Foreign Affairs* 61, no. 4 (Spring 1983), 950–70.

61 See, for example, Matthew A. Evangelista, "Stalin's Postwar Army Reappraised," *International Security* 7, no. 3 (Winter 1982/3), 110–38; and David N. Schwartz, *NATO's Nuclear Dilemmas* (Washington, DC: Brookings Institution 1983), 149.

62 *New York Times*, Friday 22 June 1984, 4.

63 For a properly sceptical assessment of Soviet conventional forces and what they could do, see John J. Mearsheimer, "Why the Soviets Can't Win Quickly in Central Europe," *International Security* 7, no. 1 (Summer 1982), 3–39.

64 Gaddis, *Strategies of Containment*, 144–5.

65 Richard J. Barnet, *The Giants: Russia and America* (New York: Simon and Schuster 1977), 106.

66 Alexander Dallin, "The Soviet Union: The Making of Foreign Policy," *Bulletin of the Atomic Scientists*, August/September 1983, 31.

67 William H. McNeill, *The Pursuit of Power: Technology, Armed Force, and Society since A.D. 1000* (Chicago: University of Chicago Press 1982), 382.

68 Deborah Shapley, "Arms Control as a Regulator of Military Technology," *Daedalus* 109, no. 1 (Winter 1980), 148; and "Technology Creep and the Arms Race," *Science*, 20 October 1978, 289.

69 Report of the Independent Commission on Disarmament and Security Issues, *Common Security: A Programme for Disarmament* (London: Pan 1982), 118.

70 LeMay, *America Is in Danger*, 93.

71 Greenwood, *Making the MIRV*, 87 and 88.

72 Randall Forsberg, "Military R and D: A Worldwide Institution?" *Proceedings of the American Philosophical Society* 124, no. 4 (August 1980), 268–9.

73 Hugh E. DeWitt, "Labs Drive the Arms Race," *Bulletin of the Atomic Scientists*, November 1984, 40.

74 Greenwood, *Making the MIRV*, 13.

75 Wolfgang K.H. Panofsky, "Science, Technology and the Arms Race," *Physics Today*, June 1981, 33.

76 Richard J. Barnet, "Annals of Diplomacy (U.S.-German Relations, Part II)," *New Yorker*, 17 October 1983, 144.

77 Herbert F. York, "Vertical Proliferation: The Nuclear Arms Race of the Superpowers," in Jack Hollander, ed., *Nuclear Energy, Nuclear Weapons Proliferation, and the Arms Race* (Stony Brook, NY: American Association of Physics Teachers 1982), 47.

78 Hans J. Morgenthau, "Some Political Aspects of Disarmament," in David Carlton and Carlo Schaerf, eds, *The Dynamics of the Arms Race* (New York: John Wiley 1975), 62.

Chapter 3

1 William L. Laurence, *Men and Atoms: The Discovery, the Uses and the Future of Atomic Energy* (New York: Simon and Schuster 1959), 268.

2 Leslie R. Groves, *Now It Can Be Told: The Story of the Manhattan Project* (New York: Harper and Row 1962), 414.

3 Jonathan Knight, "The Great Power Peace: The United States and the Soviet Union since 1945," *Diplomatic History* 6, no. 2 (Spring 1982), 180.

4 Butterfield, "Human Nature and the Dominion of Fear," 93.

5 Raymond Aron, *The Great Debate: Theories of Nuclear Strategy* (New York: Doubleday 1965; publ. in French in 1963), 15.

6 Raymond Aron, *The Century of Total War* (Boston: Beacon Press 1955), 151.

7 Melvyn P. Leffler, "The American Conception of National Security and the Beginning of the Cold War, 1945–48," *American Historical Review* 89, no. 2 (April 1984), 359–62 and 396.

8 Quoted in Richard J. Barnet, "Annals of Diplomacy," *New Yorker*, 10 October 1983, 100–1.

9 Mark Abley, "The Politics of Peace: An Interview with E.P. Thompson," *Canadian Forum*, October 1982, 39.

10 Barnet, "Annals of Diplomacy," 100.

11 P.M.S. Blackett, *Atomic Weapons and East-West Relations*, 68.

12 Aron, *Great Debate*, 15–16. In the face of those arguments that stress the political utility of nuclear weapons, especially their alleged peacekeeping functions, it might be mentioned that some observers have suggested that these weapons may well have worsened international relations and made agreements harder to reach. Blackett, for example, was of the view that nuclear weapons "had much to do with the course of the Cold War ... Though clearly serious East-West difficulties would have occurred even if there had been no atomic bombs, I do believe that their existence, and what was said and done about them, greatly intensified [these difficulties]." Blackett, *Atomic Weapons*, 69–70. If one were inclined to further speculation, and disposed to offer an alternative counter-factual argument to that which is most commonly given, it might be proposed that had the United States *not* had the atomic bomb at the end of the Second World War, an accommodation with the Soviet Union might have been achieved more readily. For in such circumstances, the USSR, having less to fear, might have been less defiant and recalcitrant, and the United States, having less to threaten with, would have been more inclined to retain more of its conventional military strength and to search harder for a negotiated postwar settlement, explicitly in terms of "spheres of influence" and perhaps a neutralized united Germany.

13 McGeorge Bundy, "The Bishops and the Bomb," *New York Review of Books*, 16 June 1983, 8.

14 Eban, *New Diplomacy*, 102.

15 Sheila Tobias, et al., *What Kinds of Guns Are They Buying for Your Butter? A Beginner's Guide to Defense, Weaponry, and Military Spending* (New York: William Morrow 1982), 173.

16 Jonathan Schell, "Reflections (Nuclear Arms Part I)," 56.

17 P.M.S. Blackett, "Military Consequences of Atomic Energy" (1948), reprinted in his *Studies of War, Nuclear and Conventional* (Edinburgh: Oliver and Boyd 1962), 15.

18 Richard Nixon, "Is Peace Possible?" *New York Times*, 2 October 1983, E19.

19 Richard Pipes, "Why the Soviet Union Thinks It Could Fight and Win a Nuclear War," *Commentary* (July 1977); reprinted in his book *U.S.-Soviet Relations in the Era of Detente* (Boulder, CO: Westview Press 1981), 135–70 (quote from 158–9).

20 "On Nuclear War: An Exchange with the Secretary of Defense," *New York Review of Books*, 18 August 1983, 30.

21 John Erickson, "The Soviet View of Deterrence: A General Survey," *Survival* 24, no. 6 (November/December 1982), 244 and 245. "In general," he argues, "the role of military power is seen from the Soviet side as a major instrument in impressing on the 'imperialist camp' that military means cannot solve the historical struggle between the two opposing social systems, at the same time reducing (if not actually eliminating) the prospect of military gain at the expense of the Socialist camp" (245). See also the authoritative and judicious discussion in David Holloway, *The Soviet Union and the Arms Race*, chap. 3.

22 See especially two articles by Raymond L. Garthoff, "Mutual Deterrence, Parity and Strategic Arms Limitation in Soviet Policy," in Derek Leebaert, ed., *Soviet Military Thinking* (London: Allen and Unwin 1981), 92–124, and "The Soviet Military and SALT," in John Baylis and Gerald Segal, eds, *Soviet Strategy* (London: Croom Helm 1981), 154–82; and Robert L. Arnett, "Soviet Attitudes towards Nuclear War: Do They Really Think They Can Win?" in ibid, 55–74.

23 Seweryn Bialer, *Stalin's Successors: Leadership, Stability, and Change in the Soviet Union* (Cambridge: Cambridge University Press 1980), 237.

24 Ibid, 257.

25 David Holloway, "Doctrine and Technology in Soviet Arma-

ments Policy," in Leebaert, ed., *Soviet Military Thinking*, 274.

26 Garthoff, in Alan F. Neidle, ed., *Nuclear Negotiations: Reassessing Arms Control Goals in U.S.-Soviet Relations* (Austin, TX: Lyndon B. Johnson School of Public Affairs 1982), 11–12.

27 Bialer, *Stalin's Successors*, 248. The Soviet interest in arms control continued to be strong. In mid-1983 two American experts on Soviet foreign policy found that "the Soviets are ready to go a long way in limiting nuclear arms. If there is equity, they are ready to talk about a warhead limitation ... as a step toward reducing the vulnerability of land-based forces. They are ready to limit missile launchers to levels significantly below those of SALT II. They are [also] ready to avoid an arms race in space and the threat this will inevitably pose to command and control, communications, and intelligence facilities." However, the U.S. government, during this period, was not in an arms control mood. Lawrence T. Caldwell and Robert Legvold, "Reagan through Soviet Eyes," *Foreign Policy*, no. 52 (Fall 1983), 18.

28 Robert G. Kaiser, *Russia: The People and the Power* (New York: Atheneum 1976), 478.

29 Stanley Hoffmann, *Dead Ends: American Foreign Policy in the New Cold War* (Cambridge, MA: Ballinger 1983), 107 and 108.

30 Kaiser, *Russia*, 463. Stanley Hoffmann points out that the USSR now has a certain stake in the status quo and a desire for a degree of predictability in world affairs, "which sharply distinguishes Soviet behavior from that of Nazi Germany. The Soviet Union, as a great power and as a stultifying bureaucracy, shows very little enthusiasm for sudden crises." *Dead Ends*, 109.

31 Kaiser, *Russia*, 453.

32 For a reconstruction of Soviet views and the reasons for Soviet missile deployments in Europe, see Raymond L. Garthoff, "The Soviet SS-20 Decision," *Survival* 25, no. 3 (May/June 1983), 110–19.

33 Marshall Shulman, in the *New York Times Book Review*, 10 July 1983, 11.

34 Peter Ustinov, *My Russia* (London: Macmillan 1983), 216 and 217.

35 Louis J. Halle, *The Cold War as History* (New York: Harper and Row 1967), 20.

36 Ibid, 24 and 25.

37 Georgi Arbatov, as quoted in Jonathan Steele, *World Power: Soviet*

144

Foreign Policy under Brezhnev and Andropov (London: Michael Joseph 1983), 25.

38 Halle, *Cold War as History*, 12.

39 Theodore H. Von Laue, "Human Rights Imperialism," *Bulletin of the Atomic Scientists*, August/September 1983, 33.

40 Halle, *Cold War as History*, 13.

41 Stanley Hoffmann, "Another 1914," *New York Times*, Sunday 18 September 1983, E19.

42 Seweryn Bialer, "Danger in Moscow," *New York Review of Books*, 16 February 1984, 8. This is a thoughtful and persuasive account of Soviet thinking in 1983–4. See also Marshall D. Shulman, "Moscow's Opportunities," *New York Times*, Sunday 10 July 1983, E21; Lincoln Allison, "Down in the Old USSR," *New Society*, 15 September 1983, 392–4; and Thomas Powers, "What Is It About?" *Altantic Monthly*, January 1984, 48–50.

43 George W. Breslauer, "Do Soviet Leaders Test New Presidents?" *International Security* 8, no. 3 (Winter 1983–4), 84 and 106.

44 Bialer, "Danger in Moscow," 6.

45 Stephen Rosenfeld, quoted in Ralph B. Levering, *The Cold War 1945–1972* (Arlington Heights, IL: Harlan Davidson 1982), 143–4.

46 Dimitri K. Simes, "How to Affect Moscow," *New York Times*, Sunday 4 July 1982, E15.

47 Simes, in Niedle, ed., *Nuclear Negotiations*, 90.

48 Stanley Hoffmann, "Detente without Illusions," *New York Times*, Monday 7 March 1983, A15.

49 Bialer, "Danger in Moscow," 8–9.

50 Michael Howard, "Nuclear Bookshelf," *Harper's*, February 1983, 70. Freeman Dyson has also drawn attention to this "failure to understand the Soviet point of view. We have never applied the diplomat's art to this most important of all diplomatic problems ... When we are deciding how to deal with the Soviet Union, either militarily or diplomatically, the first necessity is to understand the Soviet view of the world and to accept the fact that Soviet concepts and doctrines are as strong and durable as ours." "Reflections (Nuclear Weapons – Part IV)," *New Yorker*, 27 February 1984, 99–100.

51 John D. Steinbruner, "Nuclear Decapitation," *Foreign Policy*, no. 45 (Winter 1981–2), 16–28.

52 Paul Bracken, *The Command and Control of Nuclear Forces* (New Haven, CT: Yale University Press, 1983), 74–5.

53 Ibid, 64–5.
54 Ibid, 177.
55 Ibid.
56 Desmond Ball, *Targeting for Strategic Deterrence*, 37.
57 Bracken, *Command and Control of Nuclear Forces*, 241.
58 Ibid, 239.
59 Bernard Brodie, *Strategy in the Missile Age*, 378. "When relations are strained," remarked a distinguished military historian, "an ill-judged step on one side may all too easily lead to a precipitate step on the other side, and to neither drawing back for fear of losing face, at home and abroad. That is the way wars break out, more often than by deliberate intention." B.H. Liddell Hart, *Defence of the West* (London: Cassell 1950), 86.
60 Bernard Brodie, "Anatomy of Deterrence," 191.
61 Paul Warnke, in Neidle, ed., *Nuclear Negotiations*, 54. Writing at the same time, Seyom Brown expressed the view that "more than at any time in the sixty-three years of the United States-Soviet relationship, conditions are now ripe for terrible games of chicken, in which both sides have committed themselves to incompatible objectives so heavily and visibly that neither can back down without great humiliation; therefore, each becomes all the more determined to demonstrate an irrevocable commitment to persist toward its objective, in the hope that the certainty of a head-on collision will convince the *other* side to swerve out of the way first." "Power and Prudence in Dealing with the USSR," in Robert A. Melanson, ed., *Neither Cold War nor Detente? Soviet-American Relations in the 1980s* (Charlottesville, VA: University Press of Virginia, 1982), 226.
62 Alastair Buchan, "The Age of Insecurity: Some Interim Conclusions," *Encounter*, June 1963, 5.
63 John Keegan, "The Human Face of Deterrence," *International Security* 6, no. 1 (Summer 1981), 151.
64 Cyrus R. Vance and Robert E. Hunter, "The Centrality of Arms Control," *New York Times*, Sunday 26 December 1982, E13.
65 Thomas Powers, "Trying to Save Zilchburg," *New York Times Book Review*, 1 May 1983, 27.
66 Liddell Hart, *Defence of the West*, 149.
67 "Measure for Measure," *New York Times*, Sunday 4 September 1983, E14.
68 Baldwin, *The Price of Power*, 10.

69   " 'On the Brink of the Final Abyss': A Statement on War by Lord
     Mountbatten," *Defense Monitor* 9, no. 4 (1980), 4. For Robert
     McNamara's views, see his "The Military Role of Nuclear Weapons:
     Perceptions and Misperceptions," *Foreign Affairs* 62, no. 1 (Fall
     1983), 59–80. Admiral Gayler's "Opposition to Nuclear Armament"
     is published in the *Annals of the American Academy of Political
     and Social Science* 469 (September 1983), 11–21.

70   Freeman Dyson, "Reflections (Nuclear Weapons – Part III)," 76.

71   John Keegan, "The Human Face of Deterrence," 150.

72   Herbert York, *Race to Oblivion: A Participant's View of the Arms
     Race* (New York: Simon and Schuster 1970), 239. As one strategic
     expert has remarked, "there is no reason why the West should not
     undertake unilaterally those steps ... that can be afforded in terms of
     security. Indeed, unilateral arms control is probably the most
     promising approach that is left. After all, arms are designed and
     deployed by unilateral decision. It is easier to decide oneself that
     one can do away with some weapon systems or do without some
     others, than to negotiate about weapons limits with a military
     rival." Christoph Bertram, "Arms Without Control?" *Arms Control
     Today* 14, no. 8 (October 1984), 7.

73   An excellent illustration of this highly partial mode of political analysis
     may be found in a book by the philosopher Sidney Hook, *Marxism
     and Beyond* (Totowa, NJ: Rowman and Littlefield 1983), 191, where he
     is attempting to explain, especially for west Europeans who are
     contemplating the reality of Soviet power, "the nature of the deterrent
     effect of nuclear weapons. The mere presence of these weapons is
     not sufficient to deter a potential aggressor. He must be convinced of
     the will and readiness to make *defensive* use of them, otherwise they
     lose their deterrence and end up contributing to a deceptive sense of
     security. There are several ways of communicating the presence and
     strength of this will and readiness – by frequent drills accompanied by
     preparedness for civilian air defense. The paradox which seems hard
     to accept in some quarters is that the more effectively is this will and
     readiness communicated, the more likely is it that these weapons will
     never be fired." It does not occur to Hook or the many others who think
     this way that the other side has no more reason to regard these
     military displays by us as "defensive" than would we in the face of
     similar displays by them. To arrogate virtue to oneself is, no doubt, a
     common conceit, and it is no more helpful in international than in

personal relations. Another example of such non-even-handed moral evaluation appeared in a magazine supplement published on 10 April 1983, *The Present Challenge: A Report on the Nuclear Dilemma by the Cox Newspapers.* In the course of some introductory remarks, the editors observed that, "On one hand, a nuclear arsenal protects the nation's vital security and helps sustain the U.S. role in world affairs. On the other hand, nuclear weapons in hostile countries, especially Yuri Andropov's Soviet Union, threaten the existence of Americans, Soviets and everybody else on the planet Earth" (3). (I am indebted to Christine Johanson for this reference.) According to such self-regarding assumptions – and similar views are probably held by many Soviet citizens about their country – it is only the weapons of the other side that threaten, or at least threaten malevolently.

73 There are helpful remarks on these issues in Ken Booth, *Strategy and Ethnocentrism* (New York: Holmes and Meier 1979).

75 Arthur Koestler, *Bricks to Babel* (New York: Random House 1980), 519–20. The tendency to dehumanize "the enemy" is, of course, long standing. One recalls that Harry Truman, a few days after the bombing of Hiroshima, wrote a private letter to a clergyman defending his decision, and said: "Nobody is more disturbed over the use of Atomic bombs than I am but I was greatly disturbed over the unwarranted attack by the Japanese on Pearl Harbor and the murder of our prisoners of war. The only language they seem to understand is the one we have been using to bombard them. When you have to deal with a beast you have to treat him as a beast. It is most regrettable but neverthe-less true." Letter of 11 August 1945, quoted in Barton J. Bernstein, *Hiroshima and Nagasaki Reconsidered: The Atomic Bombings of Japan and the Origins of the Cold War, 1941–1945* (Morristown, NJ: General Learning Press 1975), 3.

Epilogue

1 *Khrushchev Remembers: The Last Testament* (1974), 610.
2 Dwight D. Eisenhower, "Farewell Radio and Television Address to the American People, January 17, 1961," in *Public Papers of the Presidents of the United States: Dwight D. Eisenhower, 1960–61* (Washington DC: U.S. Government Printing Office 1961), 1038–9.
3 Yergin, *Shattered Peace*, 408.

148

4 Mark Abley, "The Politics of Peace: An Interview with E.P. Thompson," 39.
5 Dyson, "Reflections (Nuclear Weapons – Part III)," 76.
6 *The Times* (London), 2 October 1981, 13.
7 E.P. Thompson, *Beyond the Cold War: A New Approach to the Arms Race and Nuclear Annihilation* (New York: Pantheon 1982), 169.
8 George F. Kennan, *The Nuclear Delusion: Soviet-American Relations in the Atomic Age* (New York: Pantheon 1982), 56–7.
9 Bertrand Russell, "Man's Peril," in his *Portraits from Memory and Other Essays* (London: Allen and Unwin 1956), 219.

Index

152